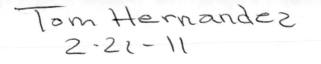

Tom Hernandez
2-22-11

D0713070

AUDEL®

Woodworking and Cabinetmaking

A Basic Guide to
Working with Wood

Materials
Design
Construction

by F. RICHARD BOLLER

Rex Miller, *Consulting Editor*

Macmillan Publishing Company
New York
Collier Macmillan Publishers
London

Macmillan Publishing Company
866 Third Avenue, New York, N.Y. 10022
Collier Macmillan Canada, Inc.

Library of Congress Cataloging-in-Publication Data
Boller, F. Richard.
      Woodworking and cabinetmaking.
      "An Audel book."
      On t.p. the registered trademark symbol "R" is superscript following "Audel"
in the series-like phrase.
      Includes index.
      1. Woodwork—Amateurs' manuals,   2. Cabinet-work—Amateurs' man-
uals.   I. Miller, Rex, 1929-
II. Title.   III. Title: Woodworking and cabinetmaking.
TT185.B67   1986   684'.08   86-2263
ISBN 0-02-512800-0

Macmillan books are available at special discounts for bulk purchases for sales pro-
motions, premiums, fund-raising, or educational use. For details, contact:

                              Special Sales Director
                              Macmillan Publishing Company
                              866 Third Avenue
                              New York, N.Y. 10022

10 9 8 7 6 5 4 3 2 1

Printed in the United States of America

Contents

Preface

This book is written specifically for the do-it-yourselfer. It is assumed that cabinetmaking projects will be carried out with limited equipment, and the instructions given are based on the use of portable electric tools and some power equipment.

Extensive information is provided concerning the materials needed and the proper design of cabinetmaking projects. The builder should become familiar with the materials and methods by reading these sections. Understanding how to use materials will make projects much easier. Functional projects can be built through proper research and design. Background information for effective planning is covered in the design section.

Acknowledgments

I would like to recognize the fine work of many students. Their cabinetmaking projects are pictured in various sections.

I wish to thank the following firms for their assistance in providing valuable illustrations and information:

American Plywood Association
Black & Decker U.S., Inc.
Delta International Machine Corporation
L. S. Starrett Company
Miller Lumber Company, Buffalo, N.Y.
Skil Corporation
Stanley Tools, a division of the Stanley Works, New Britain, Ct.
Western Wood Products Association

CHAPTER I

Material

- Common Properties
- Working with Wood
- Moisture Content
- Seasoning
- Defects
- Cabinetmaking Materials

- Softwoods
- Hardwoods
- Plywood
- Composition Wood Products
- Miscellaneous Products

From the earliest memory of man, wood has been his constant companion. Thanks to its availability and convenience, many objects have traditionally been made of wood—even early weapons, such as bows and arrows, clubs, and catapults.

In the early years of our country wood was essential. Our forefathers crossed the Atlantic in wooden ships, their goods stored in wooden containers. With their wooden tools they were prepared to establish a new frontier. See Figs. 1-1 and 1-2. The role of wood in our nation's development cannot be overestimated.

The forest proved to be a natural storehouse of materials. The hardest woods, oak and ash, were used as building material and for wagon parts, tools, and other uses. Long-lasting woods like chestnut and locust were used in foundations, and for posts and stakes. Roofs were covered with resistant cedar shingles. Ash, oak, beech, and birch were bent into parts for containers. The large sycamore made excellent hollow containers. Maple, cherry, and walnut were kept for furniture. Produce was gathered from the forest as food, and

Fig. 1-1.   Antique smoothing plane used on large surfaces.

Fig. 1-2.   Antique rabbet plane used for joints.

medicines were extracted from bark and roots. As the old adage has it, wood was used from the cradle to the coffin.

Many of our early exports came from the forests. Great quantities of oak and hickory timber were sent to the Old World for ships along with fine pine masts. Sassafras root was shipped by the boatload. With the forests as a resource, the colonies early became self-sufficient.

Today, when our natural resources are diminishing, wood is once again commanding the attention it deserves. It is the only natural resource capable of replenishing itself within our lifetime—and even more rapidly, when proper tree farming techniques are used. As we become increasingly energy-conscious, we look to wood as a material of great capabilities that requires comparatively little energy to convert it to finished products. As long as we treat it with proper consideration for growth and use, wood will continue to serve us generously.

Common Properties

In addition to being an easily obtained and renewable resource, wood has other attractions as well. It is easily worked with simple tools. Many hours can be spent carving and shaping with nothing more than a knife. Little skill is needed for basic enjoyment. Wood is a porous material that is easily fastened; gluing and clamping for permanent attachment can be quickly carried out. Fasteners such as screws and nails can be used where reuse of the material or disassembly is desired. The porosity also permits easy finishing by hand. The beautiful grain and color require no special treatment. See Figs. 1-3 and 1-4.

Wood has great strength for its weight; laminated arches and beams take advantage of this property. The wood absorbs shocks and vibrations while maintaining its structural integrity. For this reason wood is used as pillars and for railroad ties, piling, and baseball bats. Wood is also a good insulator. The many air spaces in its cellular structure create a material of very low conductivity.

Working with Wood

Working with wood requires understanding of some basic terms and processes. To cut the wood it is necessary to note the effects of the grain in the various axes. For good results both the material and the operator need to be properly oriented.

The large, flat areas on a piece of wood, whether solid or ply-

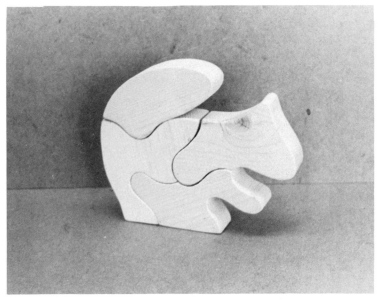

Fig. 1-3.   Softwood puzzle made with simple tools.

Fig. 1-4.   Hardwood tray emphasizes wood grain.

wood, are referred to as the surfaces. The best-looking or the flattest of the two is chosen as the face surface. The second will then be the back. In the case of square pieces a choice is still made, the only difference being the size of the surfaces.

The face is further referred to as the registration surface. See Fig. 1-5. This surface must be flat and true; when working with wood this is the first thing to check. All other areas are then squared to the registration surface.

When we talk about the other parts of a board, we may refer to them as surfaces, not to be confused with the large, flat ones. They are technically designated as edges and ends. To work with the material a registration edge must also be developed. This edge needs to be straight and true and square with the registration surface. If these two are selected, cut, and marked first, all the others can be accurately laid out and cut. These others should be true and square with the registration surface and edge.

The measurements of any board include the thickness, width, and length. They should always be listed in this specific order. They should be written as $T \times W \times L$ or $\frac{1}{2} \times 4 \times 6$, and spoken of as "one-half inch thick by four inches by six inches." This specific manner of notation is used for individual boards or workpieces. See Fig. 1-6. An object has specific measurements of its own as well: height,

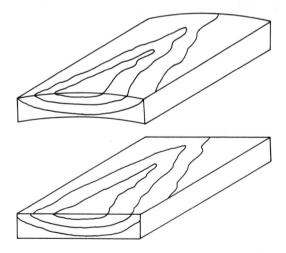

Fig. 1-5.   Identify and develop a flat registration surface from which to square all other surfaces.

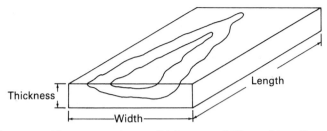

Fig. 1-6. Measurements are thickness, width, and length.

width, and depth, as in a specific piece of furniture or a house. These should not be confused with measurements of an individual board.

Attention must be given to the wood grain. The structural components of the tree create the grain, which shows up on a board as definite lines. The grain may be more or less distinctive to the naked eye, depending on the structure of the tree.

On some woods the annual rings on the end of a board may be very distinctive. The more distinct the annual ring patterns, the more distinct the grain patterns on the surface. Each wood has its own characteristic pattern. The ring growth and pore structure greatly affect the grain patterns. See Fig. 1-7.

Looking closely at the lines of grain will indicate the grain direction. It is important to see the orientation of the lines with the edge of the board. The lines may be straight, but more often they will angle up or down from the edge. This relationship with the edge determines the grain direction. For best results, cutting should be with the grain. See Fig. 1-8.

Wood should be laid out for working so that the lines of grain run the length of the board. This is necessary because the strength of wood varies in each of its three axes. Wood splits easily along the grain but is very strong across the grain. A board having long grain is much stronger. See Fig. 1-9 (p. 8).

Cutting the length of the grain is referred to as ripping. Hand tools will tend to follow the grain direction, which can be very annoying. The board will have to be turned end to end when this happens, to get a smooth cut.

Cutting across the grain is much easier than ripping. This cut severs the wood like a knife and is much easier to control when using hand tools, since grain direction needs to be considered.

Fig. 1-7. Annual ring growth and pore structure greatly affect the grain patterns.

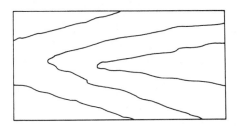

Grain Direction, Top Surface

Grain Direction, Bottom Surface

Fig. 1-8. Grain direction and relationship with the edge.

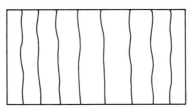

Short-Grained

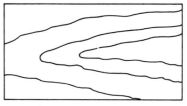

Long-Grained

Fig. 1-9. Grain running the length is much stronger.

Moisture Content

The moisture content of wood is a major factor when working with the material. Wood will shrink as it loses moisture, swell as it picks up moisture from the environment. Common methods of working with wood can never completely control the dimensional change. The woodworker must understand the effects of moisture in wood and work with it accordingly.

When trees are cut they contain a great deal of moisture or sap. Green wood is said to have from 30 percent to 200 percent moisture content. Moisture content is the weight of water in wood as compared to the weight of the oven-dry wood. Trees in North America when cut generally have 50 percent to 100 percent moisture content in the form of free water and bound water. Free water is found in the cell cavity, bound water in the cell walls. For wood to be of any use to man, the free water must be eliminated and the bound water reduced and controlled. See Table 1-1.

When all free water is gone, the wood is said to have reached the fiber saturation point. This is normally at 30 percent, and any loss of moisture below this point will be accompanied by material shrinkage. This is caused by the loss of bound water from the cell

Table 1-1. Moisture Content Scale

200%	Possible moisture content
	Free water inside cell cavity
	Bound water in cell walls
100%	Below for green wood in North America
30%	Fiber saturation point
	Free water gone
	Wood begins to shrink
20%	Below to resist decay
18%	Exterior materials for barns, fences
	Air drying sufficient
12%	
10%	Interior materials for millwork, furniture
	Kiln drying necessary
6%	

walls. As the material dries and shrinks, it increases in strength and stiffness.

Wood shrinks the most around the annual rings. See Fig. 1-10. This shows up on the tangential surface of most boards. See Fig. 1-11. The wood shrinks about 5 percent to 6 percent in this direction as compared to the green dimension. Shrinkage across the annual rings is half as much as around the annual rings. Shrinkage in the longitudinal direction is so small that it may be ignored.

Seasoning

Wood is seasoned by air or kiln drying. The wood must be properly stacked so that it is well supported and lies flat, and air can circulate entirely around. See Fig. 1-12 (p. 11). Ordinarily material is dried according to quality and ultimate use. Hard and soft woods

Fig. 1-10.   Effects of wood shrinking around the annual rings.

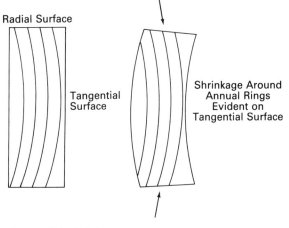

Fig. 1-11.   Tangential shrinkage.

for interior uses will be kiln-dried. The low-grade material will be air-dried or not dried at all before shipment.

Air drying is carried out by stacking outdoors. See Fig. 1-13 (p. 12). Since drying depends upon the weather and the seasons, it

Fig. 1-12. **Proper stacking ensures air circulation for drying.** *(Courtesy Miller Lumber)*

is difficult to control. While the process is inexpensive, it takes considerable time to reach low moisture contents, the final moisture content falling in the range of 12 percent to 18 percent. It is not advisable to use air-dried material for cabinetmaking. If unavoidable, special steps must be taken.

Kiln drying has several advantages over air drying. Reduction of moisture in the kiln is controlled. See Fig.1-14 (p. 13). This produces high-quality material with a low moisture content, the final moisture content falling in the 6 percent to 10 percent range. Kiln-dried material is the most reliable and best suited to cabinetmaking.

Since wood is continually losing and gaining moisture, the woodworker must know where the material has been, how it has been protected, and how it will be used. Wood products must be purchased well in advance of use. The material should be allowed to dry from several days to several weeks in the new surroundings. When the wood has gained equilibrium with its surroundings, it is suitable for use. The woodworker can then be nearly certain that registration surfaces will remain true.

Fig. 1-13. **Wood stacked for air drying out of doors.** *(Courtesy Miller Lumber)*

Defects

As wood dries and shrinks, it develops numerous defects. Most noticeable are warpage defects. *Cup* is a common warpage defect found in most boards to some extent. See Fig. 1-15. This is a curvature from edge to edge in relation to the face. To work with a board that has extreme cup, the woodworker must rip the piece down the center. See Fig. 1-16 (p. 14). The remaining pieces may be used as is, or registration surfaces developed for regluing.

Fig. 1-14. **Dry kilns used for controlled drying of wood.** *(Courtesy Miller Lumber)*

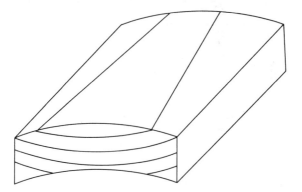

Fig. 1-15. **Cup is a curvature from edge to edge in relation to the face.**

Another warpage defect is *bow*. See Fig. 1-17. This is a curvature from end to end in relation to the face. It may be caused by irregular shrinkage or, more often, from improper support while stored. To work with a bowed board, it is necessary to crosscut it into shorter pieces. See Fig. 1-18 (p. 15). Sometimes a bowed board

Fig. 1-16. A board with extreme cup should be ripped with a band saw or hand saw to reduce the defect.

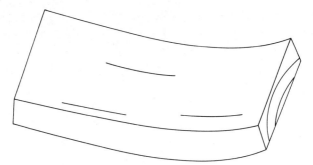

Fig. 1-17. Bow is a curvature from end to end in relation to the face.

can be bent back and attached to a stable structure with screws or nails. In edge gluing, a slight bow may be tapped down and held by the adjacent pieces.

Crook is a warpage defect that causes considerable waste in the piece. This is defined as curvature from end to end in relation to the edge. See Fig. 1-19. To work effectively with this board, a straight line is placed along the edge and cut. See Fig. 1-20 (p. 16).

A *twist* in a board is a very noticeable defect. See Fig. 1-21 (p. 17). This is caused by irregular shrinkage. The ends are not in the same plane and cuts must be made across and with the grain to get smaller, usable pieces. See Fig. 1-22 (p. 17).

Checks are a defect that must be avoided. End checks may be

Fig. 1-18. Cut a bowed board into short pieces to reduce the defect.

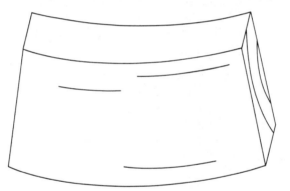

Fig. 1-19. Crook is a curvature from end to end in relation to the edge.

eliminated when laying out the rough stock. See Fig. 1-23 (p. 18). These are openings perpendicular to annual rings, caused by too rapid drying. See Fig. 1-24. To help control end checking, the ends of boards are often coated with paint or wax.

Decay is a defect often misunderstood. It is caused by wood-destroying fungi, first noticeable as a fluffy or cottony growth. The fungi feeding on the wood gradually weakens it, and it begins to crumble away. There is no such thing as dry rot; all fungi must have moisture to live, as well as sufficient oxygen and mild temperatures.

Fig. 1-20.   Eliminate crook by ripping with a band saw or hand saw to get a straight edge.

Some can conduct water as they grow. Wood will not decay unless the moisture content is continually above 20 percent.

Mold and *stain* are often referred to as decay. Usually confined to the sapwood layer, these are only superficial and do not weaken the wood. While the discoloration cannot be removed by surfacing, it is of no great consequence where appearance is secondary. However, mold and stain would be undesirable on a finished cabinet surface.

Fig. 1-21. Twist with ends that are not in the same plane.

Fig. 1-22. To get usable pieces from a badly twisted board, cut into small parts.

Other defects that affect solid wood to some degree include collapse, honeycombing, and case hardening, among others. These have not been discussed, since the general woodworker is not affected by them to any great degree. Knowledge of noticeable defects and how to work with them is most important.

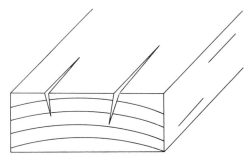

Fig. 1-23.   Checks are openings perpendicular to annual rings.

Fig. 1-24.   Cut off end checks to get a usable piece.

Cabinetmaking Materials

The selection of cabinetmaking materials will depend upon what is being built. See Fig. 1-25. For many projects softwoods will work well. These are easily purchased at local lumber yards and are very easy to work. See Fig 1-26 (p. 20). For more precise work, various hardwoods will machine better and produce a more professional-looking cabinet. The cabinetmaker's work is made much easier by the use of sheet materials, such as plywood, hardboard, and particle-board. See Fig 1-27 (p. 20).

Fig. 1-25. Coffee table made of hardwood.

Softwoods

The softwood materials available at the local lumber yard are primarily pine, fir, spruce, cedar, and redwood. These woods are produced by the evergreen (conifer) or cone-bearing tree. Softwoods are not necessarily softer or easier to work than hardwoods; two that are more difficult are yellow pine and Douglas fir. Yellow pine is used in stair treads and as tongue and groove flooring boards. Douglas fir is cut into dimension lumber, and is also the primary resource for the softwood plywood industry.

Softwood materials available are usually referred to as boards or dimension stock. The boards are thinner materials, with a thickness of less than 2 inches. These are used as shelving, facing, and trim or cut up for many woodware items. The dimension stock is material between 2 and 5 inches thick. Dimension stock is the material commonly used to build the frames of new houses, among other structures. See Figs. 1-28 (p. 21) and 1-29 (p. 22).

Softwood material is manufactured in standard sizes. Boards are usually a nominal 1 inch thick. Standard widths are 2, 3, 4, 6, 8, 10, and 12 inches. Standard lengths are 8 to 16 feet in 2-foot multiples. Dimension stock is available in a nominal thickness of 2 inches. Widths are 2, 4, 6, 8, 10, and 12 inches. Lengths are from 8 to 20 feet in 2-foot multiples. Dimension stock thicker than 2 inches is not available in large quantities or without special order. See Fig. 1-30 (p. 23).

Fig. 1-26. Softwood boards and dimension stock used to make a picnic table and benches.

Fig. 1-27. Hope chest made of hardwood plywood.

Fig. 1-28.   Dimension stock used to build the frame for new homes.

When purchasing, note that there is a difference between nominal size and actual size. Nominal size is the size by which a piece of lumber is known, e.g., 1 by 6 and 2 by 4. When the wood is cut and is green, it may be somewhat less than this size. When surfaced and dry, it has shrunk to actual size. In the example the material will be ¾ by 5½ and 1½ by 3½ inches. See Table 1-2 (p. 23).

Softwood lumber is graded according to American Lumber Standards, and grading is carried out by organizations in various parts of the country that are concerned with the products and species of their particular area. Uniform grading procedures are used to apply the standards to different species. Grading is primarily done by visual inspection and some stress testing for stiffness. Each piece is then stamped according to species and grade.

Softwoods are graded according to number and size of growth features. Boards that are available in lumber yards are divided into Finish (Select) material and Common material. The Select is further divided into grades B + BTR, C, and D. The Common is divided into grades 1, 2, 3, 4, and 5. Most lumber yards will carry only several grades in each class. See Table 1-3 (p. 24).

Fig. 1-29. A patio table made from dimension stock, pine boards, and fiberglass panel.

The boards of Select grade may all be used for finish work such as trim, woodware items, or furniture. They provide an excellent surface for all types of finish, whether natural, stain, or paint. B + BTR is the ultimate in fine appearance; many pieces would be absolutely clear. This grade is not carried by all lumber yards. C Select is only slightly inferior in appearance and usability. It is widely used for trim and cabinetwork. This grade is carried by many lumber yards. D Select is also a fine-looking grade. It is used for the same purposes as C Select where the work is generally less restrictive. In this grade one side would have a fine appearance while the back side would show numerous blemishes.

Common boards are found in five basic grades. Number 1 Common is the ultimate in knotty appearance. The knots must be small and tight. The material is suitable for knotty pine paneling. This grade is not always carried in the local lumber yard. Number 2 Common is most often used for interior trim where knotty pine lumber of good appearance is required. The knots are small and tight enough to be sealed and painted, if desired. Number 3 Com-

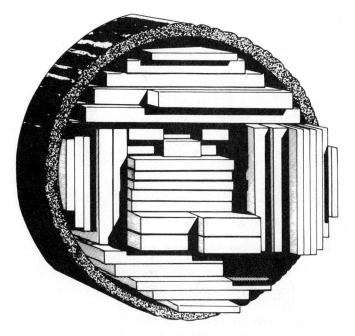

Fig. 1-30. **Boards and dimension stock sawn from the log.** *(Courtesy Western Wood Products)*

Table 1-2. **Sizes of Standard Stock**

	Nominal Size	Actual Size
	1 × 2	¾″ × 1½″
	1 × 3	¾″ × 2½″
	1 × 4	¾″ × 3½″
Boards	1 × 6	¾″ × 5½″
	1 × 8	¾″ × 7¼″
	1 × 10	¾″ × 9¼″
	1 × 12	¾″ × 11¼″
	2 × 2	1½″ × 1½″
	2 × 3	1½″ × 2½″
	2 × 4	1½″ × 3½″
Dimension	2 × 6	1½″ × 5½″
	2 × 8	1½″ × 7¼″
	2 × 10	1½″ × 9¼″
	2 × 12	1½″ × 11¼″

Table 1-3. Grades of Standard Softwood Stock

Boards	Finish (Select)	B+BTR	Ultimate appearance, clear
		C	Good appearance
		D	Good appearance, less restrictive
	Common	1	Ultimate knotty appearance
		2	Good appearance, knots
		3	Appearance with strength
		4	General use, utility
		5	Poor appearance and strength
Dimension (Light Framing)		Construction	Appearance, strength, serviceability
		Standard	Strength, serviceability
		Utility	Strength with savings
		Economy	Many defects permitted

mon is used where appearance and strength are both important. The boards may be used for shelving and paneling, among others. Number 4 Common is often known as a utility grade. It is used for general construction purposes. Number 5 Common is intended for use where a high grade is not necessary. The grade permits large defects, knots, stain, and unsound wood and is used where appearance and strength are not of basic importance.

Figure 1-31 shows a typical grade stamp of the Western Wood Products Association. This is the largest association of lumber manufacturers in the United States. Its members are located in twelve states where numerous softwoods are cut for commercial uses. The stamp signifies that the material conforms to American Lumber Standards as described in the rule book.

The information that appears on the grade stamp includes association certification mark, mill number, grade name, species, and moisture content. See Fig. 1-32 (p. 26). Of importance to the consumer is that graded lumber will provide greater uniformity and dependability. The grade, species, and moisture content become most important when working with the material.

Light framing material and studs are divided into three basic grades: Construction, Standard, and Utility. An Economy grade is often added. The material in these grades includes all species, and thickness and width of 2 to 4 inches. Construction grade is for general framing. Besides strength and serviceability, the material has good

Fig. 1-31. **Grade stamps for common pine boards.** *(Courtesy Western Wood Products)*

appearance. Standard grade is used for the same purposes, but characteristics are limited to strength and serviceability. Utility grade is recommended where both good strength and savings are desired. Economy grade allows all defects, such as large knots and holes, bark, pitch pockets, and unsound wood. While many other grade categories are used for dimension stock, the above should be of most interest to the home handyman. This material is also stamped by the official grading association. See Fig. 1-33 (p. 27).

Purchasing Softwoods

Knowledge of what materials are available is essential when purchasing lumber. The many species and grades of softwood often make selection difficult. The best approach is first to determine your needs and then consider what materials might be used. Compare price and material grade at various lumber yards. In many cases it will be necessary to visit the storage areas to see which grades they have that may be suitable. See Figs. 1-34 and 1-35 (p. 27, 28).

The softwood material will be sold by the linear foot. That is, a piece of 1 by 6 pine will be a standard price per foot of length, and a piece of 1 by 8 will be a different standard price per foot of length. A 10-foot piece will be 10 times the standard. Each grade will vary accordingly. The dimension stock is also sold by linear foot. Prices will vary a great deal, depending upon species, size of piece, grade, and locale.

Association certification mark; denotes
grading under WWPA supervision

12

Mill number, or in some cases mill
name or abbreviation

3 COM

Example of an official grade name
abbreviation, in this case no. 3
Common boards

Species mark identifying tree species,
in this case ponderosa pine and sugar pine

S-DRY

Moisture content marks. "S-DRY" indicates
M.C. not exceeding 19%; "MC 15" indicates
M.C. not exceeding 15%; "S-GRN" indicates
M.C. exceeding 19%

Fig. 1-32. Grade stamp information. *(Courtesy Western Wood Products)*

Hardwoods

The general cabinetmaker will need some hardwoods for facing, trim, and small projects. Projects made of birch-veneered plywood can be trimmed with birch or maple for an easy match. Contrasting oak facing and trim is often desired for shelving units and built-in cabinets. Poplar and willow are general-purpose hardwoods. Specialty items will call for cherry and walnut. These woods are of the deciduous type and allow precise work when cutting.

Fig. 1-33. Grade stamps for dimension stock. *(Courtesy Western Wood Products)*

Fig. 1-34. Pine boards available in common and select grades.

Fig. 1-35. Two-by-four dimension stock available in construction, standard, and utility grades.

In many cases the local lumber yard will not carry large quantities of hardwoods. A full-service lumber mill will be the primary source. Small quantities of material may be obtained from a local cabinetmaker or other such users of hardwood. Numerous craft suppliers will also list hardwoods in their catalogues.

Hardwood lumber is graded according to the amount of clear usable material in a piece, rather than number and size of defects, as in softwoods. The highest grade of hardwood lumber is Firsts and the next grade Seconds. These are sold in one grade class called Firsts and Seconds, written FAS. The material will require that 83⅓ percent of the surface yield clear-face cuttings. This material is most desirable for cabinetmaking. Common grades of hardwood will be suitable, but allow for a great deal of waste. The boards will be sold in random widths and lengths.

Hardwood is sold by the board foot. This is a standard unit of measure that is 1 inch by 12 inches by 12 inches, or 144 cubic inches. The board foot will have a definite price, based on species, grade, and milling charges. Any portion of a board foot will be based on this standard. A piece that is 1 inch by 6 inches by 24 inches would be one board foot. A piece that is 1 inch by 6 inches by 12 inches would be one-half board foot.

A simple formula is used to calculate board foot in a piece of hardwood. Board foot equals thickness in inches times width in inches times length in inches divided by 144.

$$\text{Bd. Ft.} = \frac{\text{T inches} \times \text{W inches} \times \text{L inches}}{144}$$

$$\text{Bd. Ft.} = \frac{1 \text{ inch} \times 6 \text{ inches} \times 24 \text{ inches}}{144} = 1$$

Variations of this formula are used when the width and/or length are in even feet.

When making calculations, any material under 1 inch thick is calculated as 1 inch in the formula. Material between 1 inch and 2 inches is figured to the nearest ¼ inch. Material above 2 inches is figured at its exact thickness.

Plywood

When carrying out cabinetmaking projects, the use of plywood may make the work go much faster and easier. This material consists of sheets of wood glued together, with the grain of adjacent layers arranged at right angles. The grain of the face and back run the length. See Fig. 1-36. The material is available in many types for use in and around the home.

Plywood is an engineered product made of thin layers of veneer. The cross-lamination of alternate plies produces great strength in the board. This allows for the fabrication of large pieces with strength both across and with the grain. The product is also very stable and versatile. Because the veneer is sliced from the log, the material is used more economically. Selection of face veneers can also produce a beautiful board, particularly in the case of hardwood plywood.

Softwood Plywood

Softwood plywood is made in two types, exterior and interior. The exterior has a 100 percent waterproof glueline. The interior is made with highly moisture-resistant glue. Whenever moisture is a prob-

3-Ply Construction (3 Layers of 1 Ply Each)

4-Ply Construction (3 Layers: Plies 2 and 3 Have Grain Parallel)

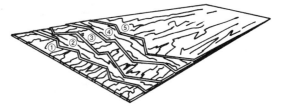

5-Ply Construction (5 Layers of 1 Ply Each)

Fig. 1-36.   Softwood plywood panel construction.

lem, the exterior type should be used. For interior cabinets and projects the interior type is sufficient.

Each type of plywood is available in a number of grades. These grades are represented by the letters N, and A through D, and indicate the veneer used on the face and back. See Table 1-4. Grades are also divided into groups according to "appearance" and "engineered" grades. The appearance grades would be of most interest to the cabinetmaker when surface appearance is important. Typical grade stamps for the material are shown in Figs. 1-37 and 1-38. For cabinetmaking purposes the A-D Interior provides good appearance on the face side for cabinets, built-ins, and shelving.

The engineered grades are designed for constructions where strength is of primary importance. Sheathing used for construction is designated C-D, or more commonly CDX, for interior with exteri-

Table 1-4. Veneer Grades Used in Soft Plywood

N	Smooth surface "natural finish" veneer. Select, all heartwood or all sapwood. Free of open defects. Allows not more than 6 repairs, wood only, per 4×8 panel, made parallel to grain and well matched for grain and color.
A	Smooth, paintable. Not more than 18 neatly made repairs, boat, sled, or router type, and parallel to grain, permitted. May be used for natural finish in less demanding applications.
B	Solid surface. Shims, circular repair plugs, and tight knots to 1 inch across grain permitted. Some minor splits permitted.
C Plugged	Improved C veneer with splits limited to ⅛ inch width and knotholes and borer holes limited to ¼×½ inch. Admits some broken grain. Synthetic repairs permitted.
C	Tight knots to 1½ inches. Knotholes to 1 inch across grain and some to 1½ inches if total width of knots and knotholes is within specified limits. Synthetic or wood repairs. Discoloration and sanding defects that do not impair strength permitted. Limited splits allowed. Stitching permitted.
D	Knots and knotholes to 2½-inch width across grain and ½ inch larger within specified limits. Limited splits allowed. Stitching permitted. Limited to Interior grades of plywood.

A-D
GROUP 1 (APA)
INTERIOR
PS 1-74 000

Fig. 1-37. **Grade stamp on sanded panel.** *(Courtesy American Plywood)*

A-B · G-1 · EXT-APA · PS 1-74 000

Fig. 1-38. **Edge stamp on sanded panel.** *(Courtesy American Plywood)*

or glue. This material will withstand considerable exposure during construction. The identification index numbers indicate the maximum support spacing for plywood in construction. Numbers on the left of the slash indicate spacing of roof framing members. Right-hand numbers refer to spacing of floor framing members. See Fig. 1-39.

Many special exterior plywoods have been developed for construction purposes. These have various surface textures and grooves to simulate individual boards. See Fig. 1-40. This exterior material works well for special projects such as a tool shed or planter. It looks good when finished with paint or stain. These plywoods are marked with grade stamps indicating the type and use of the material. See Fig. 1-41 (p. 35).

Hardwood Plywood

Hardwood plywood is used for interior cabinetry that will be stained and finished as a piece of furniture. Of most interest is the matched grain on the surfaces, which are available in birch, oak, cherry, and walnut, among others. Birch plywood is in stock at most lumber yards, with the other species available on special order.

This plywood offers the same advantages as the softwood plywood. When constructing furniture the large surfaces with beautiful, matched grain is a real asset. The material is available in various cabinetmaking grades. The core may be veneer, particleboard, or solid wood. The supplier's description of the material will indicate which is appropriate for your project.

Fig. 1-39. Grade stamp for unsanded sheathing. *(Courtesy American Plywood)*

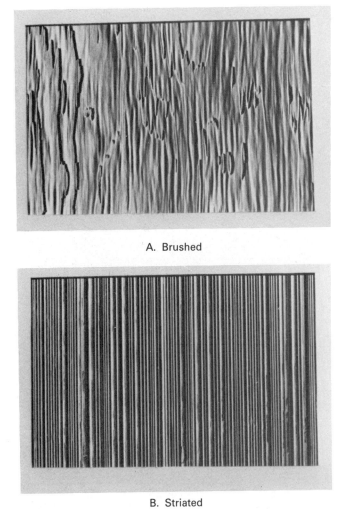

A. Brushed

B. Striated

Fig. 1-40. Examples of special exterior plywoods with various surface textures and grooves, developed to simulate individual boards.

Composition Wood Products

Particleboard is a general term used to identify a panel made by combining wood particles with resin binders and hot pressing them into a panel. This product can be engineered to develop special

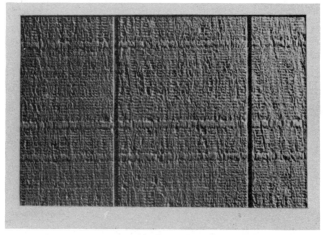

C. Kerfed Rough-Sawn

D. Texture

Fig. 1-40. *Continued.*

properties for various uses. The size and shape of the particles and the proportion of glue largely determine strength and smoothness. Increasing density will increase the strength proportionately. For interior or exterior uses, the type of glue varies to meet the panel requirements. See Fig. 1-42.

This product may be used in many places where a flat, stable panel is needed. Most often it is used as corestock for furniture,

303˚SIDING 18-S/W
T1-11
19/32 INCH
GROUP 1
16oc SPAN **APA**
EXTERIOR
PS 1-74 000
FHA-UM-64

Fig. 1-41. **Grade stamp for exterior siding.** *(Courtesy American Plywood)*

Fig. 1-42. Particleboard with varying properties and particle size.

paneling, counters, and sink tops, where it serves as the structural core and is covered with such materials as veneer, plastic laminate, vinyl, and printed materials. See Figs. 1-43 and 1-44. It is also used for partitions and shelving in cabinets. It is treated the same way as solid wood or plywood. In home construction, particleboard underlay provides a smooth surface over the subfloor for carpeting and other flooring.

Particleboard may be worked with the same tools and techniques as are used with other panel products. Standard woodworking

Fig. 1-43. Particleboard used as corestock for Formica counter-tops.

tools are sufficient. The material is easily cut, jointed, shaped, and drilled. Methods of joining parts are the same as in most cabinet-making that uses solid wood or plywood. Since the surface is smooth and flat, little preparation is needed before use.

Hardboard is a wood panel made from threadlike wood fibers that have been reunited under great heat and pressure. The natural glue in the wood cements the wood fibers into a solid panel, which is a thin, dense, strong, uniform-textured board. The introduction of chemicals and a heat-treating process further improves the board's properties. The tempered hardboard is harder and stronger and has better moisture resistance and finishing properties.

By varying the manufacturing process a number of board products may be developed. See Fig. 1-45. The board may be smooth on one side, smooth on two sides, or embossed. It may be perforated, striated, grooved, or tiled. Special finishing with paints produces wood-grained paneling, colorful enameled surfaces, or large murals.

The smooth panels are used in cabinetmaking for cabinet backs,

Fig. 1-44. Particleboard for shelving and cabinet interiors.

Fig. 1-45. A few of the available hardboard products.

drawer bottoms, and dust panels between drawers. Perforated boards work well for decorative screens and as pegboard storage surfaces. Paneling of wood-grained hardboard adds great warmth and beauty to the home. The various decorative panel products provide a highly dependable, low-maintenance surface. See Figs. 1-46 and 1-47. Worked with standard woodworking tools, hardboard is easily cut, nailed, and installed.

Miscellaneous Products

Wooden dowel is commonly used in many projects. In some cases the design of the project centers around dowel as a major part of the product. See Figs. 1-48 and 1-49. Cut into small pieces, the dowel works well as parts for games and toys. See Fig. 1-50. Dowel is also a major means of strengthening various woodworking joints.

Dowel rod is usually made of birch and is available in sizes from ⅛ to 1 inch. Standard lengths are 3 and 4 feet. Larger round stock is of pine and may be 1½ and 1¾ inches in diameter. Standard lengths are up to 20 feet.

Fig. 1-46.   Hardboard used as a drawer bottom.

Fig. 1-47. Hardboard used as a furniture back panel.

Fig. 1-48. Dowel used as members of a wine rack.

Fig. 1-49.   Stereo cabinet made with dowel and plywood panels.

Fig. 1-50.   Small parts made of dowel or round stock.

Wooden moldings are a great aid in finishing various projects. Moldings of many shapes are available in pine, with lengths up to 16 feet. See Fig. 1-51. These may be used to cover the veneer edges of plywood, trim corners, or add decorative interest. See Fig. 1-52. Moldings may also be combined to make additional shapes for decoration or for picture frames. See Fig. 1-53. Some specialty moldings are also available in hardwood.

Fig. 1-51.   A few of the typical moldings available in 250 patterns and 400 sizes.

Fig. 1-52. Pine molding used to decorate furniture.

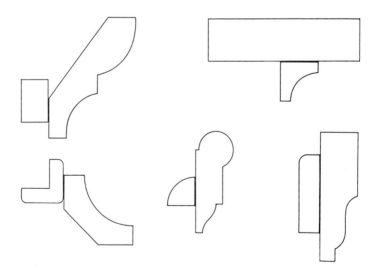

Fig. 1-53. Various moldings combined to make picture frames.

CHAPTER 2

Design

Project Selection

When deciding on home projects to build, first look at each room in the house and see where an additional piece of cabinetry will be useful. Don't forget to consider the garage and basement. Work areas such as washing and sewing areas will often benefit from additional cabinets. The object you make should satisfy a definite need. Take sufficient time to think the project through.

Study each room carefully. In many cases additional storage may be the most desirable, in the form of a closed or open cabinet. The closed cabinet is often a built-in, that is, attached to the floor and walls. A free-standing cabinet permits rearrangement of the furniture. See Fig. 2-1. Open cabinets allow for easy access to stored items. They can be built to display art items and treasures.

Any new storage unit should be planned according to the kind

Fig. 2-1.   Bookcase made with softwood plywood.

and size of items to be kept in it. See Fig. 2–2. Think of which items will be used every day, which seasonally, and which on a yearly basis. Consider, too, things that may be accumulated in the near future. Specific evaluation of needs will determine the type and size of cabinet to build.

In the case of furniture, you may wish to replace old pieces or add to existing room arrangements. In planning, be sure the room will not become too crowded. The space must allow incorporation of the new project being built. See Fig. 2-3. Try various room arrangements to include the new piece, using straight or folding chairs to simulate the space it will take up. Make sure that essential traffic

Fig. 2-2.   Pine boards glued up to make a chest.

Fig. 2-3.   Recreation room bar made with pine boards and paneling.

patterns are not disrupted and that living space does not become too crowded. Do this before planning further.

It may be desirable to build a case for storage and finish it as a piece of furniture. This works well for units below windows that may also serve as seats. Cabinets in corners and beside sofas also work well as combination units. These would be end table height. A series of cubes makes a very interesting arrangement. Open cubes with partitions may be stacked for use as furniture pieces or shelving units. A closed cube, with lid, may be used for storage of records or linens or as a bar. See Fig. 2-4. Multipurpose pieces are becoming more and more popular.

Building this type of cabinet will require the use of good-quality materials. Birch-veneered plywood for the basic case will permit easy completion of the steps to follow. Trim that matches the existing furniture may be glued on the plywood edges, corners, and face. Preparation for finishing with stain or paint will take much less time and be more rewarding if you use better wood materials.

All new pieces should be planned with attention to specific furniture types. Elements of existing pieces of furniture can be identified and duplicated, and usually include solid wood parts, trim,

Fig. 2-4.   A closed cube provides storage and table surface.

and finish. Emphasizing a specific style will help all items in a room blend together. The particular elements of various styles are discussed later in the chapter. Consideration should also be given to the style of the house. The grace and charm of an older house will look best with furniture that fits the setting. The ranch style and more contemporary structures also dictate a specific style, the A-frame being an extreme example. If the family lives in an apartment, duplex, or condominium, this will further help in choosing projects to build. Some thought should also be given to the family's future residence. As furniture pieces are added or cabinets built, their style should coordinate with others in the house. Current magazines will be a great help in deciding what kind of furniture will appear most natural.

Another consideration is the family's life-style. Types of furniture and cabinets needed vary greatly, depending on the age of family members, the life they lead, and the types of activities they enjoy. If the home is a focal point for activity and entertainment, special furniture would be desired for food serving and eating areas, and for games and hobbies. If the family participates in sports, other furniture may be needed; seasonal sports or camping and boating in summer, hiking and hunting in the fall, and winter skiing will require appropriate cabinets for storing of equipment.

During the planning stages the builder should consider the available tools. Every project will require some kind of special tools for its completion. These will range from measuring tools, hand tools, and planes to portable power tools such as the power circular saw, saber saw, and router. Many jobs will be more easily and accurately carried out with woodworking machines. Often the job done easily on a machine will require a great deal of time and effort to complete by hand. Others can be done only with special machines and cutters. Jobs with several solutions enable the builder to eliminate use of specialized machines. Advanced planning will pinpoint problem areas and help avoid pitfalls when equipment is limited.

Working space requirements are also important to a successful project. Whether the work is done in a basement, a garage, or out of doors, a sizable area is necessary. If you build large cabinets, you will need considerable space to cut the parts and assemble and finish the item. Sanding and finishing are dusty and messy and increase the space requirements still further. Suggested shop needs are discussed in another section.

Finally, consider what materials are available. Chapter 1 has provided some general information. Before starting a project, it is wise to visit local suppliers and check on the availability of the necessary material. Popular items may sometimes be out of stock. Unusual items may need to be ordered in advance. Discuss your project with an experienced woodworker to determine other solutions and the kinds of materials used in your locality. In planning projects in this book, unusual materials have been avoided.

Standard Sizes

After choosing a project, it is necessary to incorporate any standards that affect the item. Any piece of cabinetwork will have some established standard sizes. These are based upon the average body size. Furniture items have been sized for comfort and convenience. Standard heights and sizes are established with the basic purpose of the item in mind.

The standard size charts included in this book are those of most interest to the home builder. They cover general cabinetwork that many people can carry out. If items you plan to build are not covered, it would be best to look for further direction before proceeding.

Cabinets

Many different types of cabinet may be built, and for any given purpose there are many possible variations. The cabinet height chart suggests standard heights for a few of the many possibilities. See Table 2–1. Most important is to follow standard heights closely when the top surface is a work counter. This applies to desks, kitchen counters, eating counters, and other such surfaces.

The size of the cabinet may be determined by defining the purpose for which it is intended. Since the choices are so varied, it is extremely important to pinpoint the exact needs. In many cases this will be obvious from the location in the home and the space the project will occupy. Size charts are provided for night stands, chests, and dressers. See Figs. 2–5, 2–6, and 2–7 (p. 50–51). For the many other possibilities the builder will find that a good description of his needs will result in definite size specifications.

Table 2-1. Cabinet Heights

HEIGHT CHART			
24″	Base for modular shelving	40″	Secretary top
26″	Night stand	42″	Kitchen eating counter
	Bedside table	47″	Dresser
28″	Small chest		Six-drawer chest
	Tea cart		Open stereo cabinet
30″	Desk	54″	Chest with drawers
	Bathroom vanity	56″	Chest with doors
	Base units for wall furniture		
	Low eating counter	78″	Curio cabinet
	Open stereo cabinet		Wall furniture
32″	Kitchen mixing counter		Modular shelving units
33″	Bedroom dresser	80″	Bookcase
	Buffet		Modern living cases
36″	Kitchen work counter	84″	Kitchen wall cabinet
	Dry sink		
	Serving cabinet		

Wall Furniture

The use of wall furniture is an interesting method of solving storage problems while at the same time creating a beautiful living space. The units may be constructed in various widths to meet the needs of any room, large or small. They serve as desks, chests, dressers, bookcases, and display areas.

The units should be constructed with specific standards in mind. See Fig. 2–8 (p. 52). The lower units are 20 inches deep and 30 high. This depth makes possible a good work surface for a desk. The height is standard desk height and allows all units to be stacked on an even base.

The top units are 12 inches deep by 48 inches high. This depth creates a very functional shelf area, whether used with or without doors. The width of the units is engineered to suit individual room needs and may be from 2 feet to 4 feet wide.

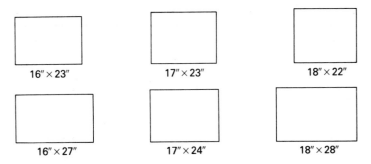

16″ × 23″   17″ × 23″   18″ × 22″

16″ × 27″   17″ × 24″   18″ × 28″

¹⁄₁₆ Scale for Comparison

Fig. 2-5.   Cabinet sizes: night stands.

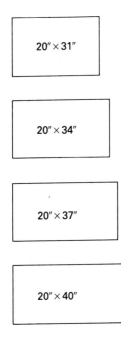

20″ × 31″

20″ × 34″

20″ × 37″

20″ × 40″

Fig. 2-6.   Cabinet sizes: chests.

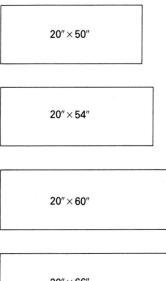

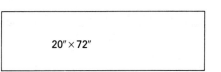

Fig. 2-7.   Cabinet sizes: dressers.

Modular Shelving Units

Modular shelving units are a modern method of solving storage problems while creating an attractive room accent. They serve as a buffet, storage cabinet, bookcase, or display area. The units are constructed to allow for rearrangement at any time. Any number of effects may be achieved with this system.

The basic units are made a standard height of 24 inches and a depth of 20 inches. See Fig. 2–9 (p. 52). The top is often covered

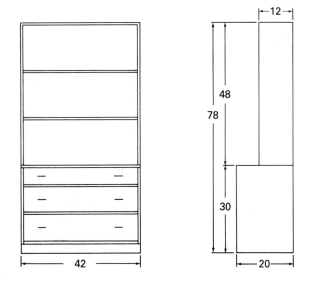

Fig. 2-8. Wall furniture.

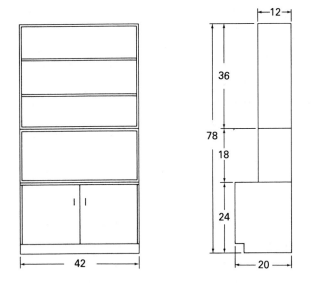

Fig. 2-9. Modular shelving units.

with Formica to allow for a multitude of uses. Doors and drawers may be used in the base units. In keeping with the modern style, all trim is square. For accent purposes a variety of materials may be incorporated. The toe space at the floor gives a suspended look. The top units are 12 inches deep to provide maximum storage. Each unit is basically a box and is of very simple construction. The boxes may be made with various designs for shelving space, or with doors of wood or sliding glass. Since they are modules, these units can be stacked one on top of the other in any order.

Cubes

This is a design specifically engineered for modern living. The construction of the cases allows for maximum flexibility while solving storage problems. The system may be used in any room in the house and may be rearranged at any time. Space is used to greatest advantage with a series of cases stacked vertically to provide needed storage. See Fig. 2-10. They may also be positioned horizontally, two or three high, to provide shelving and dresser space.

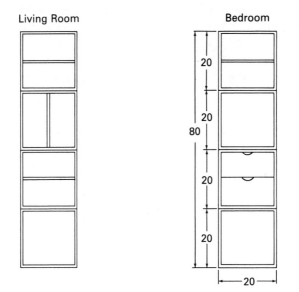

Living Room   Bedroom

Fig. 2-10.   Modern living cases.

The cases are 20-by-20-inch cubes of simple construction. The cubes are built with wide or narrow shelves, partitions, or drawers. They can be used to store or display any item from books to stereo components. Finished with various accent colors, the cases lend great interest to a room. See Chapter 8 for construction plans.

Vanities

The cabinet height for a vanity is laid out to be 30 inches. To this the ¾-inch-thick Formica or ceramic top is added for a 30 ¾-inch total. This is a comfortable height for the average man or woman. The cabinet height may be adjusted to change the overall height. An inch or two up or down may prove more practical for some families.

The cabinet depth is determined from the top size. The standard counter surface is 22 inches deep, for both preformed and Formica tops. This dimension may also be varied according to the space available. Where space is at a premium, more shallow units may be constructed with smaller sinks.

During construction the cabinet sides are laid out by working backward from the top size. A ¾-inch overhang is desired at the cabinet front. This makes the cabinet plus facing a total of 21¼ inches deep. The facing is usually of ¾-inch-thick material. The

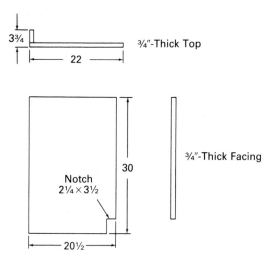

Fig. 2-11.   Vanity layout.

plywood cabinet side then becomes 20½ inches wide. See Fig. 2-11. In the cabinet side the notch for the toeboard is cut 2¼ inches deep by 3½ inches high. With the facing attached, the notch becomes 3 inches deep.

The width of a vanity depends upon the space available. Wide countertops are desirable as long as they do not get in the way of house doors or cause traffic problems. A ¾-inch overhang on each edge is preferred. Be sure that there is enough space in the bathroom to open the vanity doors wide.

Basic vanity shapes have been provided to help in planning. See Fig. 2-12. The wider cabinets allow for drawers on either side of the sink. A face board is placed in front of the sink that matches the style of drawer fronts. This board is normally 17 inches wide for an average sink. See Chapter 8 for construction plans.

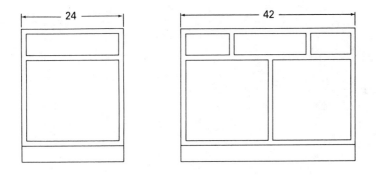

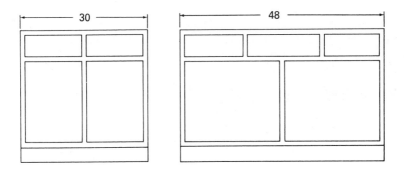

Fig. 2-12.   Basic vanity shapes.

Kitchen Cabinets

Kitchen cabinets are built at a standard height of 34½ inches. With the addition of the 1½-inch-thick top, the overall work height is 36 inches. Standard heights should be closely followed for other kitchen surfaces, such as mixing counters, high or low eating counters, and planning centers. Kitchen cabinet depths are 24 inches, including the facing. The standard counter depth is 25 inches. See Fig. 2-13.

The upper kitchen cabinets should also incorporate appropriate standards. Most important is to maintain the desired clearance between the work counter and the upper cabinet. A maximum height is observed so that shelf space can be easily reached. See Fig. 2-14. The unused portion to the ceiling is built in, with a drop ceiling. Cabinets above the sink, range, and refrigerator are shortened to provide additional clearance. All cabinets are 12½ inches deep including the facing. See Chapter 8 for construction details.

Platform Beds

The platform bed is a project that can easily be carried out by the home craftsman. In designing the project it is necessary to first

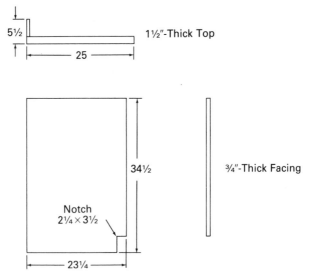

Fig. 2-13. Kitchen cabinet layout.

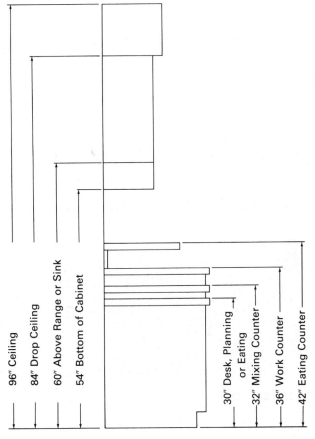

Fig. 2-14.   Kitchen cabinets: work heights and clearances.

determine the size desired and the height of the platform. See Fig. 2-15. The bed sizes conform to standard mattress sizes. The choice of height allows for a modern or high platform. The platform bed provides a very solid sleeping surface. An additional advantage is the large space underneath the bed for storage drawers.

The platform is basically constructed as a plywood box. Beds larger than single size are constructed in identical halves to facilitate handling and moving. They are screwed together side by side when in use. Openings in each half allow for large storage drawers. These are supplied with metal side guides to carry the weight of stored items. A decorative headboard may be attached to the platform. See Chapter 8 for construction details.

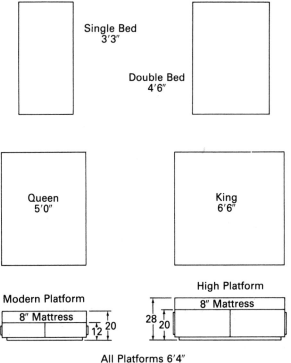

Single Bed
3'3"

Double Bed
4'6"

Queen
5'0"

King
6'6"

High Platform

Modern Platform

8" Mattress

8" Mattress

28 20

12 20

All Platforms 6'4"
from Head to Foot

Fig. 2-15. Bed sizes.

Tables

When planning to make a table the builder has many options. Once a specific need and type of table is decided upon, some further decisions can be made. The height chart shows various types of tables and their desired heights. See Table 2-2. A coffee table falls in the range of 16 to 17 inches. Modern tables will have the lowest heights, to conform with other modern furniture. Other coffee tables will fall at the upper end of the range. Each type of table has suggested heights based on ultimate use.

A further option concerns the size of the table. Standard sizes for coffee and end tables appear in the size layout charts. See Fig. 2-16 (p. 60). The size you choose depends on how much space is

Table 2-2. Table Heights

HEIGHT CHART		
16″ Cocktail tables ↓ and 17″ Coffee tables	26″ Game tables ↓ and 27″ Card tables	
19″ Smoking stand ↓ and 21″ Pedestal tables	29″ Dining room ↓ and 30″ Kitchen tables	
24″ Lamp tables ↓ and 25″ End tables		

available for the table and the use to which it will be put. A very convenient size of small coffee table is the one measuring 18 by 42 inches. This size fits well near a small sofa without becoming an obstacle in the room.

A round table often best fits the available space. These tables utilize corner space well and require a relatively small area. See Fig. 2-17 (p. 61). In addition to blending with other furniture, round tables allow easy movement around them. See Fig. 2-18 (p. 62).

A final decision is the type of base the table should have. The framework is an open structure and may be a pedestal, trestle, or leg and rail construction. The type of table will often dictate the type of base needed. A trestle type of base or a leg and rail structure will work well with the small coffee table. Various types of pedestals work well with a round table.

Design Fundamentals

When planning a project to build, consideration must be given to fundamentals of design, which include function, appearance, and structure. Each project, whether you are building an original item, changing or copying an existing item, or using a combination of ideas from various sources, must be evaluated in terms of how it will function, how it will look, and how it will be built. As the project takes form in your mind, write down ideas that satisfy these basic fundamentals as they apply to the specific project.

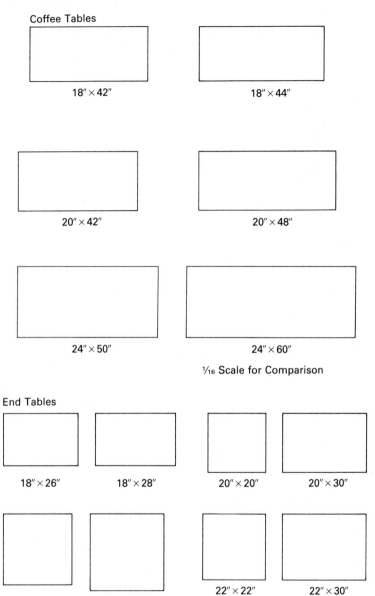

Coffee Tables

18″ × 42″

18″ × 44″

20″ × 42″

20″ × 48″

24″ × 50″

24″ × 60″

¹⁄₁₆ Scale for Comparison

End Tables

18″ × 26″

18″ × 28″

20″ × 20″

20″ × 30″

24″ × 24″

26″ × 26″

22″ × 22″

22″ × 30″

¹⁄₁₆ Scale for Comparison

Fig. 2-16. Table sizes.

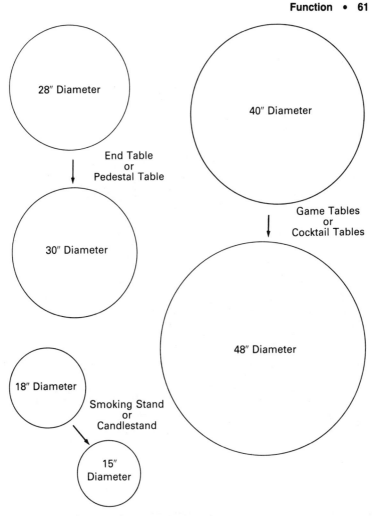

Fig. 2-17.   Occasional table diameters.

Function

Any project worth making must function as intended. You may find it very easy to identify the functions of a project, or you may need to list the basic functional requirements on paper. This is extremely important regardless of whether the item is large or small. As your

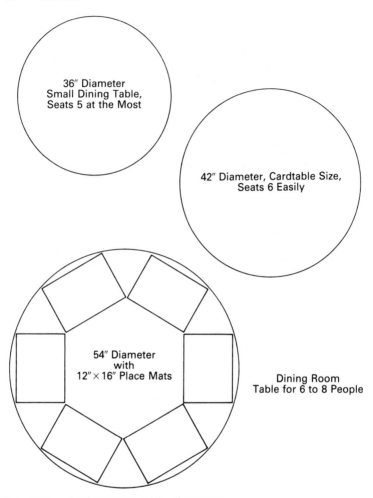

Fig. 2-18. **Dining room table diameters.**

woodworking projects become more complex, for storage, work, or multiple functions, this becomes a key in planning.

A simple one-step stool, for example, has several functional requirements that must be kept in mind. These relate to its intended use and the people using it. The stool must be the proper one step up. This is usually about 8½ inches. It must be wide enough to support the feet and not tip. You might also want to consider ease of moving and storage as part of the function. These ideas may take any of several forms when the stool is complete. See Figs. 2-19, 2-20, and 2-21 (pp. 64–65).

A bookcase must accommodate the size books you own. For general use this dictates shelves at least 12 inches apart and at least 8 inches deep. Shelves smaller than this are ineffective for general use. This attention to function is necessary whether the bookcase is a series of shelves attached to the wall, an open structure, or a closed case.

Furniture items and cabinets have standards that must be followed. The height, width, and depth can easily be identified from references. Standards for those projects of interest to the general cabinetmaker have been included here. To pinpoint other functional requirements, consider your needs. Details such as type of trim, shelves, doors, drawers, and other elements can then be planned accordingly.

Appearance

Any piece of cabinetry worth making must be pleasing to look at. A definite *furniture style* must be chosen for any piece being constructed. Selected elements of each style can be incorporated in the cabinetry. Depending on individual preferences, the style may be traditional, Early American, or contemporary, among others. The style will dictate the exact form the cabinet will take and suggest shapes, materials, and colors to use. The elements of various furniture styles are discussed below.

A pleasing design is also aided by attention to basic design principles. Good *proportion* must be built into the furniture piece. Proportion is the relationship of the parts of the project to one another. Designers agree that the overall area of a rectangle is in better proportion than a square, the prime example being the golden mean rectangle. In this rectangle the short side is .618 of the long side. With some variance this is used as a guide to accommodate furniture styles and personal needs. Cabinets, chests, and tables built in this relationship are pleasing to the eye.

Individual parts of a project must also be in the proper proportion. The style chosen often dictates this size relationship of parts. A common mistake is making legs too small and spindly. Continue

Fig. 2-19.   Step stool with slanted support.

Fig. 2-20.   Step stool with straight support.

Fig. 2-21. Step stool with built-in handle.

to look at well-made furniture pieces and pictures to develop a feeling for this relationship.

Good *balance* is also necessary in design. When an object appears to be at rest it is said to have good balance. This principle is demonstrated in many things in nature. A large man with small feet and thin legs seems to be out of balance. Balance may be achieved by placing his feet further apart. In this case, we have *formal balance:* the arrangement of the parts is symmetrical.

Informal balance is achieved by arranging various-sized objects so that they appear in balance. Placing a large picture on the wall with two smaller pictures beside it makes an arrangement that is in balance. This is referred to as informal balance: the objects are not symmetrical.

When the materials with which a project is made go well together, it has *harmony.* Again the furniture style dictates color and the various types of materials to use. A combination of materials will look good in various styles when handled properly. Care must be taken, however, not to overdo the use of different materials.

Rhythm is a design principle expressed by repetition of shape, color, and design details. When a design shape is used on the top edge of a cabinet, it should be repeated on the base apron. Straight-line designs are repeated in contemporary projects, in others curved designs are incorporated. Do not use too many different shapes in one piece. Keep the design as simple as possible.

Emphasis is a design principle easily accomplished in woodworking by the placement of grain patterns. Certain additional materials, colors, and shapes provide emphasis in some furniture styles; hardware may provide further emphasis. Care must be taken not to construct a conglomeration with too many points of interest.

The cabinetmaker should look at his design idea and see that it satisfies these five design principles. Proportion, balance, harmony, rhythm, and emphasis should be noted in the plan. This will make the piece pleasing in appearance to many individuals.

Structure

Thinking about how the project will be built requires many decisions. The project needs to serve its function, look attractive, and be structurally sturdy. To carry out this phase successfully the builder must understand construction materials and methods. If you have not already done so, scan these areas of the book to get basic ideas.

Select materials that seem appropriate for your project. Plywood, solid wood, and a variety of other materials are possibilities. Select those that will make a definite contribution. Each material should be chosen for a specific reason and be suitable to the furniture style chosen. Do not attempt to substitute inexpensive materials that will detract from the beauty of the project.

After selecting materials, be sure they are used honestly. Use each where its outstanding properties will be taken advantage of. Use plywood for large surfaces, solid wood for trim, less expensive wood for cabinet interiors, plastic for serviceability, metal for strength and accent. Do not attempt to make materials do what they are not intended for. Lay out solid wood pieces with the grain running the length of the piece. Use pieces thick enough to appear pleasing.

Proper selection of joints and accurate machining is essential. The project must be made so that it will last for many years. Select joints so that they will not interfere with one another. Cut them properly so that they will add strength and not decrease it. In many cases, this will mean cutting joints only halfway through a given piece.

Furniture Styles

When identifying projects to make, the builder must determine a furniture style. Each style possesses definite features that can be identified and incorporated into the new piece. Every piece in a given style is made with the appropriate materials and finished in the tones of that style.

Certain styles are long lasting, others are transient. Six basic and important styles are traditional, Colonial or Early American, Italian provincial, French provincial, Spanish or Mediterranean, and modern or contemporary. Other styles the builder might like to

Fig. 2-22. Decorative trim and base curves on Early American cabinet.

work with are Danish, Scandinavian, Oriental, and Shaker, among others. These are much more subtle, but they do have definite, identifiable elements.

Many features of the various styles are difficult for the builder to duplicate without special tools and equipment. The styles most often copied are Colonial or Early American, modern or contemporary, and Spanish or Mediterranean.

The early settlers in America developed furniture to meet their everyday needs. These pieces were made by local craftsmen with native woods. With the available cherry, maple, pine, and oak, they made sturdy utilitarian pieces. Parts were often carved or turned and assembled with pegs and wedges. Finishes incorporated the medium brown stains.

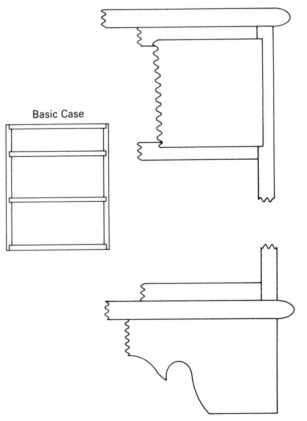

Basic Case

Fig. 2-23. **Early American bedside table.**

Colonial furniture, influenced by pieces from Europe, was somewhat more ornate. This set the trend for more delicate and decorative pieces.

Today, Early American furniture is made of pine, cherry, or maple. The style features turnings. Often the turnings will incorporate the "vase" shape. Chests and cabinets incorporate decorative trim and base curves. See Fig. 2-22 (p. 67). With appropriate trim a bedside table can be made to fit in many settings. The cases drawn are made of birch plywood with maple trim. See Fig. 2-23.

An Early American case is given the appropriate rounded edge. The base curves are distinctive. The Colonial case features sculptured legs and more decorative trim. See Fig. 2-24.

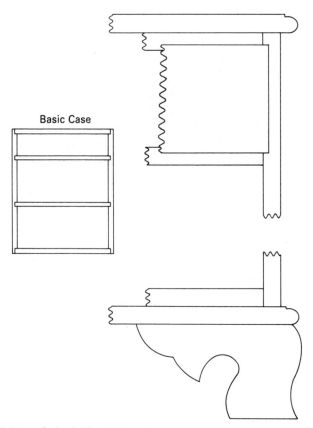

Basic Case

Fig. 2-24.   Colonial bedside table.

Modern or contemporary furniture has a clean, simple look. Pieces are functional and informal. Many are often used for a variety of purposes. Various materials are incorporated, such as glass, metal, and plastics. The emphasis is on the beauty of the material, with no added decoration.

The bedside tables show the effectiveness of simplicity. They are made of birch plywood with maple trim. See Fig. 2-25. Simple straight-line design is featured, with a straight tapered leg. The second case features a clean front with hidden drawer pull. The base is an open skeleton with mortise and tenon attaching rails to turned legs. See Fig. 2-26.

Spanish or Mediterranean furniture features the use of many

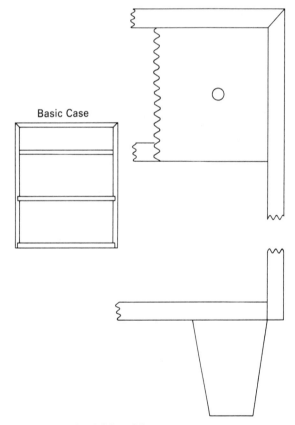

Fig. 2-25.   Modern bedside table.

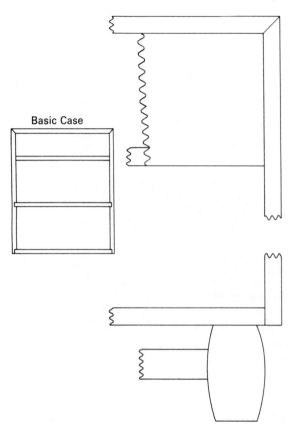

Fig. 2-26. Contemporary bedside table.

geometric shapes. The designs are adapted from Gothic architecture. The furniture is heavy and is made from pecan or oak wood. A wide variety of materials are used, including metal, ceramics, wrought iron, and glass. The finish usually includes a dark stain.

The Mediterranean bedside table is made of birch plywood with oak trim. See Fig. 2-27. Geometric shapes are incorporated on the drawer front. The drawer pull adds to this effect. The drawing shows the effect of heavy trim on the basic case. See Fig. 2-28.

Simple changes in construction and trim have made the basic case a distinctive piece of furniture. When constructing any piece, the builder can duplicate special features of existing furniture. The project then will harmonize with the other furniture in the room.

Fig. 2-27. Heavy trim and geometric shapes in Mediterranean cabinet.

Project Planning

Specific planning begins after making a definite selection and choosing a furniture style. Now information must be gathered concerning the actual piece. This relates to sizes, style elements, materials, construction methods, and finish. Basic information can be found in this book. Other references will be of value in determining what the project will look like. Furniture examples can be seen in stores and magazines to further stimulate the imagination.

With a note pad, pencil, and measuring tape in hand, visit local furniture stores to examine items similar to your selection. Make sketches noting general configuration and possible sizes. Identify elements of the style that you think can be duplicated in the home shop. Make sketches of these details so that later drawings can be

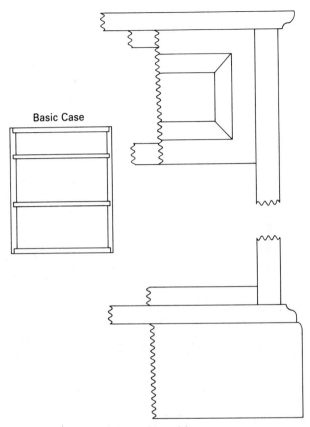

Basic Case

Fig. 2-28.   Mediterranean bedside table.

easily produced. In some stores a catalogue is available that will be of great help in planning.

For final size information, consult the tables in this book that list acceptable standards. First study the height charts available for cabinets of this type, then look at the related size layouts provided. You should by now have pinpointed the exact sizes in which you want to construct your project.

Suppose you have decided to make a night stand of Early American design to match pieces already in use. The cabinet height chart indicates that a height of 26 inches is standard. The size layouts show 16-, 17-, and 18-inch-deep cabinets of various widths from 23

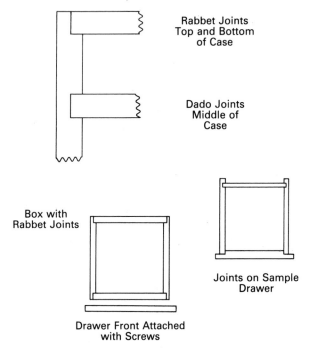

Fig. 2-29. Preliminary sketches of joints.

to 28 inches. Select a size that will fit your needs and the space available.

While inspecting commercial items you should look at materials and construction techniques. Special materials will often be used that are not available locally. These might include plywood panels of appropriate size with edging as an integral part, or special thickness particleboards or back panels. You should use more standard materials that can be easily obtained and not attempt to duplicate these special materials. A little more money spent on materials is a sound investment and will go a long way in producing a quality piece of cabinetry.

While industrial methods will not be exactly the same as those followed in the home shop, they will be of interest for the sake of comparison. Check the methods of assembly to see what types of joints have been used. Unusual joints may be of advantage in mass assembly in industry, but not appropriate for the cabinetmaker to try to duplicate. Note where screws and nails have been used in assembly. Determine what methods were used in applying trim and attaching various other parts. See how drawers are constructed and what type of drawer runners are used. Remember, there may be simpler and easier ways for you to do these jobs with outstanding success.

Begin preliminary sketches, incorporating all the information you have gathered. Refine the sketches you made previously and pinpoint ideas that look promising. See Fig. 2-29. The basic shape of the cabinet should be drawn, with attention to height of base, shelves, and drawer. See Fig. 2-30. Details should be noted for possible trim shapes to use for the top edge, apron, and base. See Fig. 2-31. There will be many possibilities from which to choose. A good rule of thumb is to stick to similar trim shapes; in this case the top edge and the lower apron will have the same shape. When planning trim be careful not to overdecorate. This is a major mistake of many builders.

Sketches should be refined by the use of a grid placed behind the sketching paper. See Fig. 2-32. You may easily make a grid by placing ¼-inch-spaced lines on a paper. These lines will show through the drawing paper. This technique will help in developing sketches to scale. The ¼-inch grid can be easily used to represent ½ inch or 1 inch in actual size. See Fig. 2-33 (p. 77).

When all decisions have been made concerning the project, make drawings with straightedge and ruler. If a T square, triangles, and drawing board are available, use these for more accuracy. Select

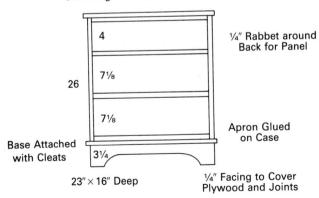

Fig. 2-30. **Preliminary sketches of basic case.**

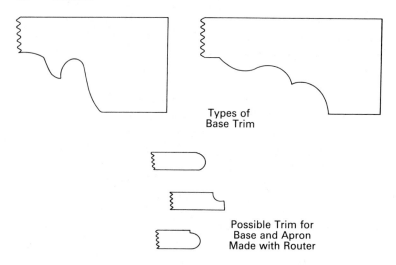

Types of
Base Trim

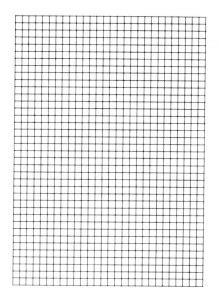

Possible Trim for
Base and Apron
Made with Router

Fig. 2-31.   Preliminary sketches of trim.

Fig. 2-32.   Grid.

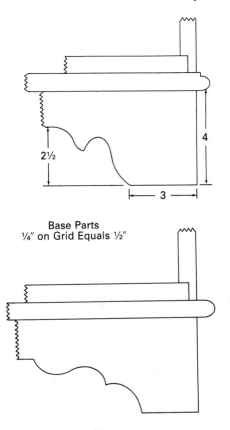

Base Parts
¼″ on Grid Equals ½″

Fig. 2-33.   Sketching with grid.

the appropriate scale for your size of paper, possibly using one-quarter or one-half, as you did when sketching. These drawings will become a paper exercise in construction. See Figs. 2-34, 2-35, and 2-36. You will need to determine material sizes, locate pieces accurately, and draw joints as they will actually be cut. If you plan efficiently and accurately on paper, you will have fewer problems in actual construction.

After you have finished drawing, develop a materials list. See Table 2-3 (p. 80). This list should indicate the kinds of material needed, the size of pieces cut from each kind, and the number of pieces. This list will give a total for each kind of material to help in purchasing. The list will also be used when cutting parts to exact

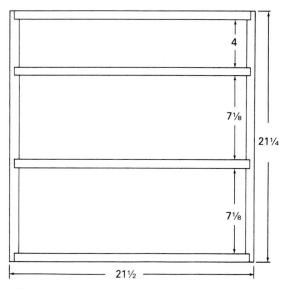

Fig. 2-34.   Night stand joint structure.

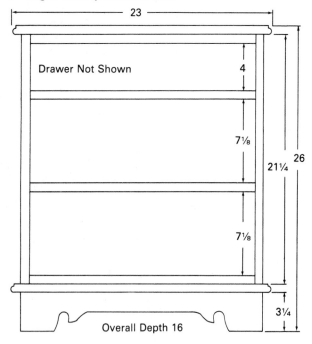

Fig. 2-35.   Night stand, front view.

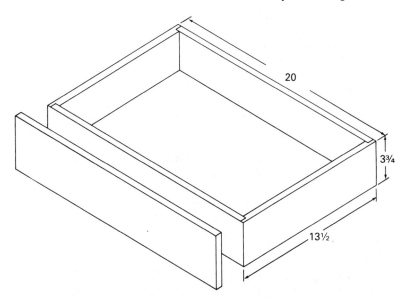

Fig. 2-36. Box with drawer front attached.

size when building the project. When determining sizes, be sure to make allowance for pieces that will go into joints. When purchasing, consider extra material for the rough cutting of parts and for sawing and smoothing on the edges. A material list is included that explains how material sizes were derived. See Table 2-4. If this step is carried out thoroughly and accurately, the building activity will proceed with ease.

The final step in planning is a full-sized pattern of the night stand base trim. The drawing can be developed from sketches made while gathering information. Normally the front center is 1½ to 2½ inches off the floor. The foot area that contacts the floor is from 3 to 4 inches wide. The base trim is usually 4 inches high. Plan the curved decoration based upon these specifications.

Cut a piece of paper to the size of the board as indicated on the material list. Lay out the above specifications. Sketch the desired design, concentrating on one end. Make smooth, flowing curves to complete the design. Fold the paper in half and cut opposite ends from your sketch at the same time.

When construction begins, start with the basic case and build on this. Cut pieces for the case from the birch plywood. Cut joints for the side and back. After gluing the case, trim the face with the

Table 2-3. Night Stand Material List
Dimensions listed are finished size.

Case		
Sides	2 pc. ¾″ × 15″ × 21¼″	Birch plywood
Shelves	4 pc. ¾″ × l4¾″ × 20¾″	Birch plywood
Trim	2 pc. ¼″ × ¾″ × 21¼″	Birch
Trim	4 pc. ¼″ × ¾″ × 20″	Birch
Top		
Board	1 pc. ¾″ × 15¼″ × 21½″	Birch plywood
Trim	1 pc. ¾″ × ¾″ × 23″	Birch
Trim	2 pc. ¾″ × ¾″ × 16″	Birch
Apron		
Front	1 pc. ¾″ × 2½″ × 23″	Birch
Sides	2 pc. ¾″ × 2½″ × 16″	Birch
Base		
Front	1 pc. ¾″ × 3¼″ × 21½″	Birch
Sides	2 pc. ¾″ × 3¼″ × 15¼″	Birch
Corner blocks	2 pc. 1½″ × 1½″ × 3″	Spruce
Cleats	3 pc. ¾″ × ¾″ × 13″	Spruce
Back		
Panel	1 pc. ¼″ × 20¾″ × 21¼″	Birch plywood
Drawer		
Sides	2 pc. ½″ × 3¾″ × 14″	Pine
Front, back	2 pc. ½″ × 3¾″ × 19½″	Pine
Front trim	1 pc. ½″ × 4½″ × 20½″	Birch
Bottom	1 pc. ¼″ × 13½″ × 19½″	Hardboard
Screws	21 pc. 1¼″ #8 flat head	
Handle	1 pc.	

Table 2-4. Night Stand Material List

Case	
Sides	¾″ × 15″ × 21¼″
	(The 15″ width allows for ¼″ trim on the box and ¾″ apron on front for overall 16″ depth)
Shelves	¾″ × 14¾″ × 20¾″
	(Shelves are ¼″ less than the width of sides to allow for back, 20¾″ length allows for ⅜″-deep joints into sides)
Trim	¼″ × ¾″ × 21¼″
Trim	¼″ × ¾″ × 20″
	(Nailed and glued on front to cover plywood and joints in case)

Table 2-4.–*Continued*

Top
  Board   ¾″ × 15¼″ × 21½″
                           (Width allows for ¾″ trim for overall cabinet depth of 16″, length allows for ¾″ trim on edges for total of 23″)
  Trim   ¾″ × ¾″ × 23″
  Trim   ¾″ × ¾″ × 16″
                           (Allow slightly more than finished length for cutting of miters)

Apron
  Front   ¾″ × 2½″ × 23″
  Sides   ¾″ × 2½″ × 16″
                           (Width of 2½″ allows for glue surface under case; allow slightly more than finished length for cutting of miters)

Base
  Front   ¾″ × 3¼″ × 21½″
                           (Length shortened to allow apron to overhang ¾″ on each side)
  Sides   ¾″ × 3¼″ × 15¼″
                           (Length shortened to allow apron to overhang ¾″ on the front)
  Corner blocks   1½″ × 1½″ × 3″
                           (Square up pieces of 2 × 4 material)
  Cleats   ¾″ × ¾″ × 13″
                           (Predrill in two directions to attach to base and apron)

Back
  Panel   ¼″ × 20¾″ × 21¼″
                           (Width of panel is length of shelves to fit in back rabbet)

Drawer
  Sides   ½″ × 3¾″ × 14″
                           (Width allows easy fit in cabinet opening)
  Front, back   ½″ × 3¾″ × 19½″
                           (Length allows fit in cabinet opening and into ¼″ joint in drawer sides)
  Front trim   ½″ × 4½″ × 20½″
                           (Attached to box drawer with ¼″ overhang on all sides of opening)
  Bottom   ¼″ × 13½″ × 19½″
                           (Size allows for ¼″-deep groove on all sides of drawer to fit bottom)

Screws   1¼″ #8 flat head
                           (To attach apron to bottom of cabinet and cleats to base trim and apron)

Fig. 2-37.   Basic case glued with skeleton frames.

Fig. 2-38.   Basic case trimmed with ¼″-thick pieces.

desired pieces. See Figs. 2-37 and 2-38. Cut trim and glue to the top. Cut trim for the apron. Shape trim for the apron and on the top. Attach top and apron pieces with screws. Make base parts, cut decorative design on the front, and attach with cleats. The drawer is the last thing to be constructed and is carefully fitted to the cabinet. This kind of construction is very similar to building a house, that is, adding parts to the basic unit until completion. Consult the other chapters of this book for techniques of construction.

CHAPTER 3

Hand Tools

- Safety Rules for Hand Tools
- Measuring Tools
- Layout Tools
- Cutting Tools
- Shaping Tools
- Drilling Tools
- Assembly Tools

Working with hand tools can be most rewarding. To have created an item with your own hands is a source of great pride and satisfaction. A wide variety of projects can be carried out with a few hand tools and some selected portable power tools. As your interest and experience grow, you can add to your workshop.

The hand tools in this section have been grouped into categories. Each tool is illustrated, with information about its use. Typical operations are pictured and discussed.

Use of hand tools necessitates acquiring attitudes and habits that lead to safe operation. The woodworker must know the proper procedures well enough to follow them automatically. If you do not, stop work and think about the safe habit to follow. This will create a safe atmosphere for work. Remember, you are protecting not only yourself but others.

Read the following list of rules for the safe use of hand tools. The list is presented in a sequence that should make sense as you approach a job. Keep the rules in mind as you work.

Safety Rules for Hand Tools

Have your safety glasses ready as you begin work.

Use the correct tool for the job.

Have your tools in good condition, and sharp.

Follow proper procedures when using tools, and cut away from your body.

Carry tools properly, hold them with the points down, and don't place them in your pockets.

Use special tool carriers for jobs outside or where you move around a lot.

Don't move rapidly from place to place carrying tools.

Have the work securely held with clamps or a vise.

Don't allow tools to pile up as you work.

Keep the work area free of scraps and accumulations of sawdust.

Store tools in racks with the points down and sharp edges turned away from the direction of grasp.

Keep tools from rusting and corroding by cleaning with steel wool and waxing.

Measuring Tools

The following are measuring tools that are most often needed by cabinetmakers and for home use:

Bench rule
Folding rule
Steel tape rule
Long tape
Calipers
Dividers
Compass

Fig. 3-1.   Bench rule. Maple rules with graduations of 8ths on one side and 16ths on the other, available in 1- and 2-foot sizes. *(Courtesy Stanley Tools, a division of the Stanley Works)*

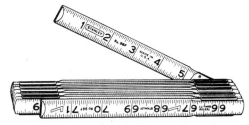

Fig. 3-2. Folding rule with easily folded spring joints, readable from the inside, 6-foot length. *(Courtesy Stanley Tools, a division of the Stanley Works)*

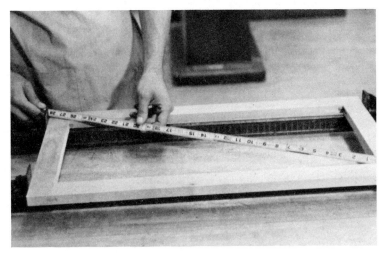

Fig. 3-3. The folding rule works well for inside measurements.

Fig. 3-4. Steel tape rule. Provides long, faster measurements; wide blade stays rigid for a long reach; has easily operated thumb lock. Rules are available in metric measure and in various lengths. *(Courtesy Stanley Tools, a division of the Stanley Works)*

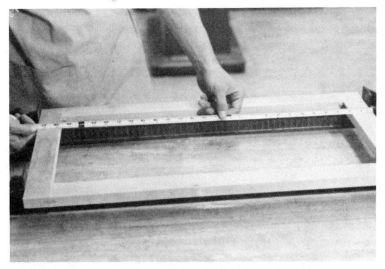

Fig. 3-5. The steel tape hooked on the edge for outside measurements.

Fig. 3-6. Steel tape. A wide stainless-steel tape for long measurements, used for foundation and house frame layout, available in 50- and 100-foot lengths. *(Courtesy Starrett)*

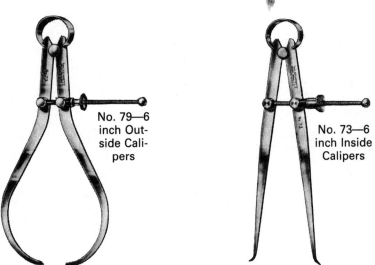

No. 79—6 inch Outside Calipers

No. 73—6 inch Inside Calipers

Fig. 3-7. Inside and outside calipers for measuring diameters, specifically during lathe turning. *(Courtesy Stanley Tools, a division of the Stanley Works)*

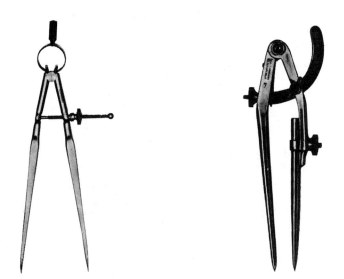

Fig. 3-8. Dividers, used to step off measurements and divide a distance into equal parts. One leg is removable, to use with a pencil. *(Courtesy Stanley Tools, a division of the Stanley Works)*

Fig. 3-9. Tin cans can often replace a compass to lay out various curves.

Layout Tools

The following are layout tools that are most often needed by the cabinetmaker and carpenter:

Try square
Combination square
T bevel
Carpenter's square
Aluminum level
Awl
Chalk line

Fig. 3-10. Try square. Lays out and measures 8ths, for testing squareness of individual parts and adjacent pieces in a structure. *(Courtesy Stanley Tools, a division of the Stanley Works)*

Fig. 3-11.   Using a try square to check end squareness.

Fig. 3-12.   Combination square. Blade with graduations of 8ths, 16ths, and 32nds, movable head with scratch awl and level. Has a wide variety of uses. *(Courtesy Stanley Tools, a division of the Stanley Works)*

Fig. 3-13.   Use of the squaring head on the combination square to locate a line parallel to an edge.

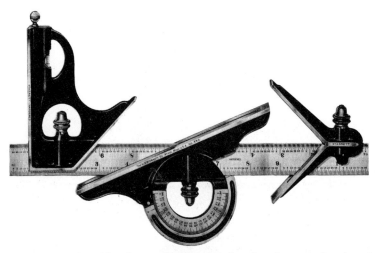

Fig. 3-14. Combination set with squaring head, centering head, and protractor head, for all types of layout work. *(Courtesy Starrett)*

Fig. 3-15. Use of the protractor head on the combination square to lay out an angle.

Fig. 3-16. **T bevel with blade locking device, for layout and transfer of angles and testing cuts.** *(Courtesy Stanley Tools, a division of the Stanley Works)*

Fig. 3-17.   The protractor head used to set the T bevel.

Fig. 3-18.   Carpenter's square with long tongue and blade to check squareness of large pieces. Has many uses in working with plywood. *(Courtesy Stanley Tools, a division of the Stanley Works)*

Fig. 3-19.   Aluminum level, to check level and plumb. Available with replaceable and adjustable vials. *(Courtesy Stanley Tools, a division of the Stanley Works)*

Fig. 3-20.   Scratch awl with sharp point for locating drill locations and scribing lines. *(Courtesy Stanley Tools, a division of the Stanley Works)*

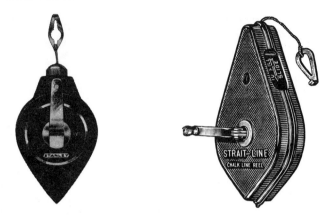

Fig. 3-21. Chalk line, for marking the layout lines in house construction and roofing. *(Courtesy Stanley Tools, a division of the Stanley Works)*

Cutting Tools

The following are cutting tools that are most often needed by cabinetmakers and for home use:

Crosscut saw
Back saw
Coping saw
Keyhole saw
Dovetail saw
Hacksaw
Miter box

Fig. 3-22. Crosscut saw. A panel saw with crosscut teeth, 26 inches long with 8 points per inch, for general use. *(Courtesy Stanley Tools, a division of the Stanley Works)*

Fig. 3-23. Back saw, a fine-toothed saw with crosscut teeth. The thin blade and stiff back permit cutting of wood joints and other accurate work. *(Courtesy Stanley Tools, a division of the Stanley Works)*

Fig. 3-24. Small parts held on a bench hook and cut with the back saw.

Fig. 3-25. Coping saw, for cutting curves, externally and internally, after inserting blade through a hole. Blade may be rotated to any position and reversed. *(Courtesy Stanley Tools, a division of the Stanley Works)*

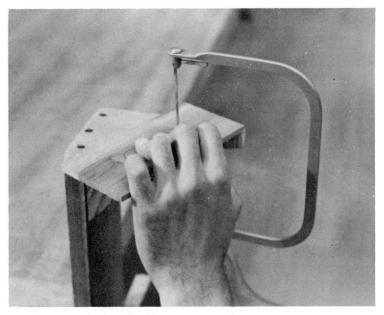

Fig. 3-26. A coping saw used to cut small curves. Hold stock on a "V" board and place blade with the teeth pointing toward the handle.

Fig. 3-27. Keyhole saw, for cutting holes and small openings. A saw nest may be purchased that includes blades of various shapes and tooth coarseness, with interchangeable handle. *(Courtesy Stanley Tools, a division of the Stanley Works)*

Fig. 3-28. Dovetail saw, easy to control for fine cabinet work and cutting of wood joints. Extremely fine teeth and thin blade. *(Courtesy Stanley Tools, a division of the Stanley Works)*

Fig. 3-29. Cutting a joint with the dovetail saw.

Fig. 3-30. Hacksaw with rigid frame adjustable for 8″, 10″, and 12″ blades; allows blade to face in four directions.

Fig. 3-31.   Mini hack, extra versatile and convenient for many hacksaw jobs. Uses regular hacksaw blade or broken blades from 3½" long. *(Courtesy Stanley Tools, a division of the Stanley Works)*

Fig. 3-32.   Making a flush cut with the mini-hacksaw.

Fig. 3-33.   Miter box for cuts of any angle from 45° to 90°. Adjustable stops to control depth of cut.

Shaping Tools

The following are shaping tools most often needed by cabinetmakers and for home use:

Surform tools
Wood files
Draw knife
Spokeshave
Chisels
Gouges
Block plane
Smooth plane
Router plane
Cabinet scraper
Hand scraper
Paint scraper

Fig. 3-34. Surform tools. Plane, pocket plane, and round file used for fast cutting and forming of wood, soft metals, and plastics. *(Courtesy Stanley Tools, a division of the Stanley Works)*

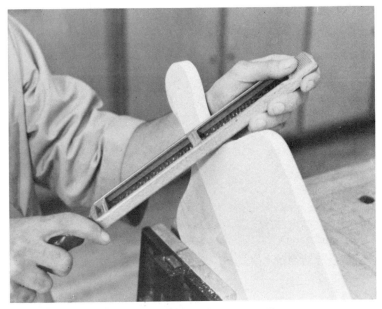

Fig. 3-35.   Use of a surform file to form a handle.

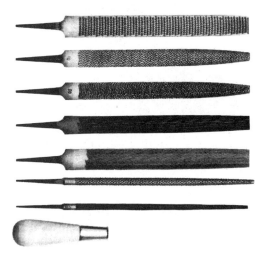

Fig. 3-36.   Rasps and wood files in half-round and round contour for fine shaping.

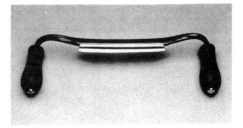

Fig. 3-37. Draw knife for carving and shaping, removes material quickly from deep concave areas.

Fig. 3-38. Spokeshave, used in carving and shaping, to smooth concave surfaces. *(Courtesy Stanley Tools, a division of the Stanley Works)*

Fig. 3-39. Chisel, used for cutting joints and shaping. Use by hand or with a mallet. In widths from ¼″ to 1½″. *(Courtesy Stanley Tools, a division of the Stanley Works)*

Fig. 3-40. Using a butt chisel with the bevel up to smooth a joint. Note that work is held securely.

Fig. 3-41. Using a butt chisel with the bevel down to remove material quickly. Note that work is held securely.

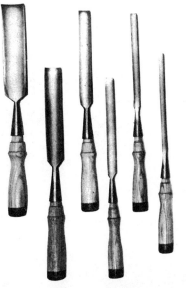

Fig. 3-42. Wood gouges for carving and sculpture.

Fig. 3-43. Block plane for cutting end grain and other small jobs. Cutter is at low angle with the bevel up. *(Courtesy Stanley Tools, a division of the Stanley Works)*

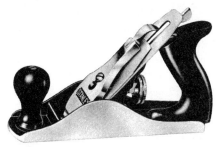

Fig. 3-44. Smooth plane with 9¾" base, for general use. Longer planes available for special purposes. *(Courtesy Stanley Tools, a division of the Stanley Works)*

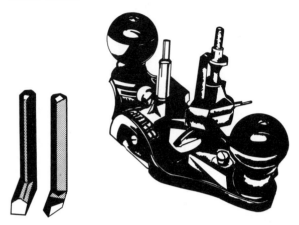

Fig. 3-45a. Router plane for leveling grooves and joints cut by hand.

Fig. 3-45b. Router plane used to level the bottom of a joint. Note that work is held securely.

Fig. 3-46. Cabinet scraper, used to produce a fine surface on furniture pieces. Thumbscrew allows adjustment for fine or coarse shaving. *(Courtesy Stanley Tools, a division of the Stanley Works)*

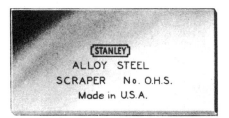

Fig. 3-47. Hand scraper, a versatile tool used to produce a fine surface on furniture pieces. Hardened steel blade. *(Courtesy Stanley Tools, a division of the Stanley Works)*

Fig. 3-48. Producing a smooth surface with a hand scraper. *(Courtesy Stanley Tools, a division of the Stanley Works)*

Fig. 3-49. Paint scraper, used to remove excess glue and paint.

Drilling Tools

The following are drilling tools most often needed by cabinetmakers and for home use:

Hand drill
Twist drill bit
Countersink
Brace
Auger bit
Expansion bit
Yankee drill

Fig. 3-50. Hand drill with ¼″ capacity. Three-jaw chuck holds small twist drills.

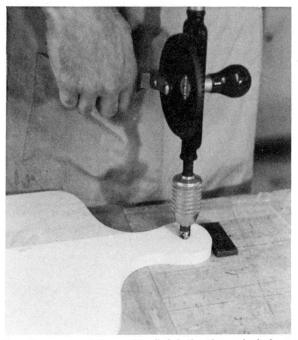

Fig. 3-51. A countersink used to finish the thong hole in a cutting board.

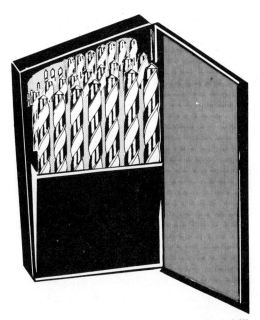

Fig. 3-52. Twist bit set with ¼″ shanks for hand drill and electric drill.

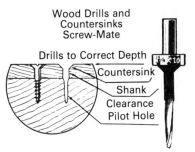

Fig. 3-53. Screw-mate set for drilling pilot, shank, and countersink holes for accurate assembly.

Fig. 3-54. Countersink for use with brace. *(Courtesy Stanley Tools, a division of the Stanley Works)*

Fig. 3-55.   Countersink for use with hand drill, electric drill, or drill press. *(Courtesy Stanley Tools, a division of the Stanley Works)*

Fig. 3-56.   Rachet bit brace for use with square taper shank bits and small and medium-size drills. *(Courtesy Stanley Tools, a division of the Stanley Works)*

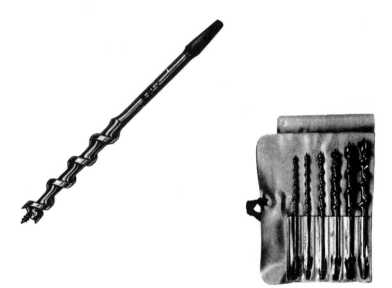

Fig. 3-57.   Auger bit for boring holes with the brace. Screw tip pulls bit into the wood. Available in sizes ¼″ to 1″.

Fig. 3-58. Expansion bit for boring large holes with a brace. Holes from 1″ to 2″, with other cutters available.

Fig. 3-59. Yankee drill, uses eight drill sizes, stored in handle when not in use. Drills with push-pull action. *(Courtesy Stanley Tools, a division of the Stanley Works)*

Assembly Tools

The following are assembly tools most often needed by cabinet-makers and for home use:

Claw hammer
Nail set
Wonder bar
Screwdriver
Spring clamp
Bar clamp
Web clamp
Corner clamp

Fig. 3-60. Claw hammer, all-steel hammer of rigid construction, with vinyl grip. A 16-oz. hammer is good for general use. *(Courtesy Stanley Tools, a division of the Stanley Works)*

Fig. 3-61. Nail set for placing nail heads below the surface and completing hard-to-reach nail jobs. *(Courtesy Stanley Tools, a division of the Stanley Works)*

Fig. 3-62. Wonder bar, for pulling, prying, lifting, and scraping, complete with nail slot at both ends. *(Courtesy Stanley Tools, a division of the Stanley Works)*

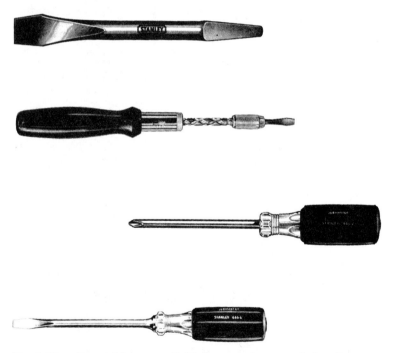

Fig. 3-63. Screwdrivers, available in many types and sizes for specific applications. *(Courtesy Stanley Tools, a division of the Stanley Works)*

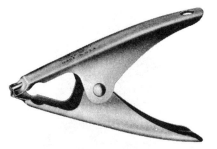

Fig. 3-64. The spring clamp is useful for gluing in place small parts, such as cleats or trim pieces.

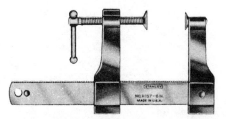

Fig. 3-65. Bar clamp, adjusts to approximate size and screws tight. Available in various lengths. *(Courtesy Stanley Tools, a division of the Stanley Works)*

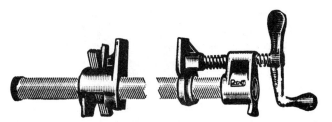

Fig. 3-66. Set of fixtures used on ¾″ pipe to make any length of bar clamp.

Fig. 3-67. Web clamp, holds irregular shapes with even pressure. Tightens with wrench or screwdriver.

Fig. 3-68. Web clamp used on irregular surfaces.

Fig. 3-69. Corner clamps, ideal for gluing miter joints. Rigid cast construction for accuracy. *(Courtesy Stanley Tools, a division of the Stanley Works)*

Fig. 3-70.   A corner clamp used when assembling miter joints.

CHAPTER 4

Machines

- Radial Arm Saw
- Table Saw
- Jointer
- Band Saw

The use of woodworking machines will make many cabinetmaking operations very easy, permitting greater accuracy with little effort. Each machine has a specific purpose and is designed for certain jobs. Use the tool or machine that will best carry out each job; do not try to use a machine on a job for which it is not suited.

Only four machines are covered in this section. These are the radial arm saw, table saw, jointer, and band saw. A great number of machines may not be available to the home craftsman, but one or several of the machines listed and a few portable electric tools will allow most projects to be carried out with success.

As you prepare to work with each machine, become familiar with its use and care. Consult the manufacturer's specifications for proper setup of the machine. Follow their suggestions for safe use. The following is a list of safety rules for various machines:

Work on the machine alone; your undivided attention is essential.

Do not wear loose clothing or other articles; wear protecting footwear in the shop; tie or cover long hair; do not wear jewelry.

Use safety glasses, ear protection, and face mask when necessary.

Have a clear understanding of the task before beginning work.

Make sure the machine is in proper working order.

Do not use a machine with dull blades.

Set up the machine properly before turning on the power.

Have push sticks handy.

All machine guards should be in place and working properly.
Note: In the illustrations in some cases guards have been
removed to get clear photographs.

Be aware of danger zones around the blade and where kickback
can occur.

Always reach around or over the blade area; do not move your
hand through the area near the blade.

Allow the machine to come to full speed before cutting.

Have the work area clear of tools, boards, and waste materials.

Turn the machine off when the cut is complete. Do not allow
it to run when it is not needed or unattended.

Keep the machine in good running order by checking manufacturer's instructions for maintenance and care.

Clean and protect shiny metal surfaces by applying paste wax
with steel wool and buffing.

Radial Arm Saw

The radial arm saw is one of the most versatile pieces of equipment
available to the home owner. See Fig. 4-1. In selecting equipment
to purchase, the radial arm saw is easily the first choice. The saw
can make all basic crosscutting and ripping cuts. It will cut rough
stock, make finish cuts, and cut joints. With the addition of various
accessories it will also act as a jointer, a shaper, and a sander, among
other functions. See Fig. 4-2.

The machine is convenient to use. The arbor is above the table
and is easily adjusted for the various cuts. In many operations the
board does not need to be moved and is held stationary against the
table fence. This is the case in crosscutting operations. The cabinetmaker will find that most of the work he needs to do on the
radial arm saw will be crosscutting. The basic cuts described will
therefore be of this kind. Rip cuts to break down large pieces can
easily be done with the portable circular saw, as described in Chapter 5. It is recommended that ripping be done in this way. Additional

Fig. 4-1. A typical 10-inch radial arm saw.

CROSSCUTTING   MITERING   SURFACING

SHAPING   DADOING   DRUM SANDING

Fig. 4-2. Various cuts made with the radial arm saw. *(Courtesy Black & Decker)*

uses of the radial arm saw are covered in the manufacturer's instructions concerning use of the saw.

The size of the saw is determined by the largest blade it can use. The 10-inch saw accommodates a 10-inch-diameter blade, and will cut to a depth of 3 inches. Use the appropriate diameter of blade for the machine and be sure it has the right-sized arbor hole to fit the arbor. The same type of blades that are used on the table saw can be used on the radial arm saw. Since it does mostly crosscutting, have available both a crosscut blade and an all-purpose combination blade.

Other important parts of the radial arm saw include the table and fence; yoke, motor, arbor, collar, and nut; and overarm and column. The table should be made of a stable material, such as plywood or particleboard. A covering of ¼-inch-thick hardboard is desirable to keep the principal table from being cut. The hardboard can be held with small brads and is easily replaced when worn. The fence should protrude at least ¾ inch above the table surface. It should be made of a straight wood piece, which should be replaced frequently for accurate and safe cuts. The yoke is movable in a 360-degree range for great versatility. The motor is tilted in the yoke to any angle desired. The blade is placed on the arbor with the appropriate collar and nut. The overarm is raised and lowered with the elevating crank to control the depth of the cut. The column provides support and allows pivoting of the overarm for various miter cuts. Safety devices available on the radial arm saw are the blade cover with anti-kickback mechanism, blade guard, and brake.

Basic adjustments are very easy to make on the saw. Make sure the blade is perpendicular to the table. See Fig. 4-3. Place the square in the saw blade gullets, not against the teeth. To adjust, remove the plate on the bevel pointer and loosen the outside socket head screws. Tilt the motor so that it is tight against the square, and tighten screws firmly. Replace the cover. Crosscut travel may also have to be adjusted square with the fence. To adjust, loosen the arm clamp and set screws. Place a steel square against the fence to check the blade as it is moved forward. See Fig. 4-4. Make adjustment with screws to move the overarm left or right. Lock the adjustment screws and recheck with the square. Test these two basic adjustments by making a cut on a wide board. Consult the owner's manual for basic setup and other, more complicated adjustment instructions.

Fig. 4-3.   Checking saw blade squareness with the table.

Fig. 4-4.   Checking saw blade travel square with the fence.

To change a blade, turn off all the power and disconnect the cord. Raise the arm until the blade clears the table groove. Remove the blade cover and guard. Use the wrenches provided with the saw. One wrench will hold the arbor from turning. Hold this wrench in place and brace it against the.table. Use the second wrench to loosen the arbor nut by turning clockwise. Change blades, making sure the new blade has teeth pointing in the direction of the motor rotation. (The teeth will point down toward the table.) Replace the collar and nut. Tighten the nut counterclockwise with wrenches. Replace the blade cover and guard.

When cutting, several safety rules not listed in the introductory section apply specifically to the radial arm saw:

> Be sure the yoke is locked in the back position when you start work and finish.
>
> When preparing to cut, hold yoke handle, unlock yoke, and turn on the power—in that order.
>
> Hold board securely against fence, pull yoke forward slowly; hold back slightly, since the saw tends to feed itself.
>
> Never get your hands near the blade; maintain the 4-inch margin of safety.
>
> When crosscutting material on the left, hold with your left hand and pull the yoke with the right; when crosscutting material on the right, hold with the right hand and pull the yoke with the left. This will prevent your body from crossing in front of the blade.
>
> Make sure the table is clear of sawdust and chips to ensure proper support of the workpiece.
>
> Support properly all pieces being cut by the use of additional devices.
>
> Return yoke to back position when cut is complete, lock in place, turn off power, and brake blade to a stop.

The crosscutting action is carried out with the board held securely against the fence. Both trim cuts and cuts to finished lengths are easily performed:

> Adjust the saw so the blade is ⅛ inch below the table surface for a finish cut.
>
> Hold work securely against the fence, with the hand on the same side as the material.
>
> Hold onto the long part of the material, with the hand well back from the blade.

For an accurate start, place layout line on the board in relation to a new cut in the fence. See Fig. 4-5.

While holding securely, pull yoke slowly forward to complete the cut as desired. See Fig. 4-6.

Return yoke to back position, and secure by locking.

Crosscutting of wider pieces of plywood can be done by following a line and cutting in from both edges of the plywood.

Crosscutting of thicker blocks, above the 3-inch capacity, can be done by cutting halfway through the piece, turning it over, and completing the cut from the other side.

Crosscutting of duplicate parts, small pieces, and miters are also easily done. Extra care must be taken to hold the workpieces.

Duplicate parts are easily cut by clamping a stop on the fence. See Fig. 4-7.

Proceed to cut as in any normal crosscutting operation.

Several duplicate parts may be cut at once by clamping a board flat on the table and perpendicular with the fence.

Fig. 4-5. Line on board in relation to cut in fence.

Fig. 4-6. Slowly advance yoke to complete cut.

Fig. 4-7. Crosscutting duplicate parts with a stop.

Small pieces are cut in a normal crosscut fashion by cutting
from a larger board, which is easily held.

When cutting duplicate small pieces, proceed with caution.
Pieces may be held in place with a push stick so they will
not jump or pinch when the yoke is pushed back.

Miters are cut by turning the overarm to the necessary angle.
See Fig. 4-8.

Locate the part in relation to the trial cut in the table or fence.

Hold securely and proceed slowly to get a smooth, accurate
cut.

Dado joints can be easily done, the same way as crosscutting.
To get the desired depth of cut, raise the overarm. A few joints can
be cut with a single blade by making multiple passes. For many
joints the dado head makes the job simple and quick.

Place the dado head on the arbor, as with standard blades. The
collar will not be used when a wide dado is desired.

Set up dado head as with the table saw, and tighten the nut.

Replace blade cover and guard.

Fig. 4-8.   Crosscutting a miter.

Make a trial cut in stock of equal thickness to the good board. Check width and depth of cut.

Align workpiece with the cut in the fence and slowly proceed to cut. See Fig. 4-9.

Hold work securely and pull yoke forward slowly and carefully, since a great deal of material is being cut away.

Cutting dadoes on the radial arm saw permits accurate cuts and clean edges on the workpiece.

Carefully and slowly back out of the dado to maintain a clean cut. A slight pressure to the left or right may be helpful.

A stop dado can be cut by stopping the yoke at the proper location. See Fig. 4-10.

A machine stop clamp on the overarm will aid in cutting stops uniformly.

Dadoes can be cut at an angle. See Fig. 4-11.

The operation may cause the workpiece to creep; hold it securely or clamp board to the table.

Proceed as with other dado cuts.

For operations other than these for general cabinetmaking, consult the manufacturer's books concerning use of the saw. Decorative cuts that would require a molding head on the radial arm saw can be done on the router, as can groove and rabbet joints with the

Fig. 4-9.   Cutting a dado joint on the radial arm saw.

Fig. 4-10. Cutting a stop dado.

grain. Many ripping operations can also be done more safely on the table saw.

Table Saw

The purpose of the table saw is to crosscut and rip stock, and to cut joints. See Fig. 4-12. The saw is available in various sizes. See Fig. 4-13. A 10-inch tilting arbor table saw is good for most general-purpose work. Table saws are available in floor or bench models. The bench models would have an additional advantage for the home owner. See Fig. 4-14. It may be placed on a movable bench or base, so it can be pushed out of the way when not in use. Which kind to purchase depends upon the amount and type of work that will be done.

The size of the saw is determined by the diameter of the blade it uses. The diameter affects the blade's capacity to cut above the table; a 10-inch blade can cut 3¼ inches above the table. Make sure the blade used is the appropriate diameter for the machine and has the right-sized arbor hole.

Many different types of blades are available; some are general purpose, others for specific jobs only. A crosscut blade is useful

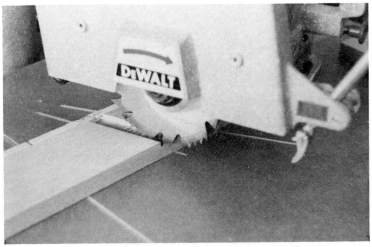

Fig. 4-11. Cutting a dado at an angle.

Fig. 4-12. Ten-inch tilting arbor table saw.

Fig. 4-13.   Twelve- to fourteen-inch tilting arbor table saw.

when a smooth cut is desired for end grain joints, such as miters. A 10-inch crosscut blade would have approximately 100 teeth. Combination blades are available for use in any situation. These are referred to as the all-purpose combination and the chisel-tooth combination. Both have relatively large teeth, a 10-inch blade having approximately 40 teeth. This type of blade gives a good cut when crosscutting and ripping. A carbide-tipped blade is also available with 40 teeth. This blade is more expensive, but it does all general-purpose work and stays sharper longer. The dado set is used for wide grooves and dadoes. It normally includes two outside saws and five inside chippers.

Other important parts of the table saw include table and insert; miter gauge and fence; arbor, nut, and washer; guard and hand wheels. See Fig. 4-15. The table is the machined work surface. Make sure this is bolted parallel to the blade surface when attached. The

Fig. 4-14.   Ten-inch bench model tilting arbor table saw.

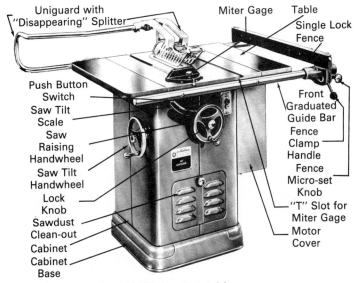

Fig. 4-15. Parts of a 10″ tilting arbor table saw.

blade extends through the table insert. The miter gauge runs in a table slot, the fence on guide bars. The fence must be adjusted parallel to the grooves machined in the table. The blade is mounted on the arbor with the appropriate nut and washer. The guard covers the blade while cutting is done. Some guards include a splitter to keep the kerf open, and anti-kickback fingers. Other guards do not touch the wood. The guard should be used at all times, except when making special cuts where it may interfere or the mounting may be in the way. The front handwheel raises the blade, and the side handwheel tilts it. Consult the manufacturer's instructions for special features of your saw and setup and adjustment instructions.

To change a blade, turn off all power and disconnect the cord. Remove the guard and table insert. Wedge the blade with a board to keep it from turning. Use the special arbor wrench to loosen the nut. See Fig. 4-16. Pull it toward you. Take off the nut, washer, and blade. It is a good idea to run the nut and washer onto your finger so as not to drop it in the sawdust. Replace the blade with the teeth pointing toward you. Install the washer and nut. Tighten the nut with the wrench while holding the saw blade by hand, making sure it is properly aligned. Put the table insert and guard

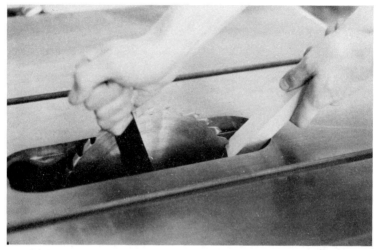

Fig. 4-16. Wedge blade and loosen nut with an arbor wrench.

in place. Connect the power. Make sure the blade used is intended for the job to be done.

When cutting, several safety rules not listed in the introductory section apply specifically to the table saw:

> Have the blade adjusted ⅛ inch above the work.
> Have guard in place and adjusted before power is turned on.
> Use boards with two registration surfaces. Place one on the table and the edge against the guide.
> Always use saw guides; don't work freehand.
> Stand to the left of the blade to operate.
> Be sure blade does not touch any metal parts.
> Use the necessary push sticks.
> Keep the material securely against the guides.
> Pass material completely past the blade when cutting.
> Support long pieces properly.
> Do not cut short pieces—less than 6 inches—on the table saw.

Ripping stock is cutting with the grain, which is necessary to get pieces with parallel edges. The fence is used as a guide when ripping.

Select a combination blade for most ripping jobs.

Measure from a tooth of the blade set toward the fence. Add
$\frac{1}{16}$ inch for future smoothing on the jointer.

Put guard in place.

Cut the good piece between the fence and blade. The waste is
on the outside of the blade.

Slightly cut the board, remove, and measure it to check the
setting.

Move slowly past the blade to cut.

Keep securely against the fence. See Fig. 4-17.

Use push sticks if the board is less than 4 inches wide.

Move completely past the blade with push sticks or by hand.
See Figs. 4-18 and 4-19.

Crosscutting stock is cutting across the grain of the wood to
square the ends of a board and cut desired lengths. The miter gauge
is used as a guide for crosscutting.

Select a combination or crosscut blade.

Put guard in place.

Make a trial cut to check squareness of the miter gauge.

Fig. 4-17. Holding workpiece against fence with push sticks.

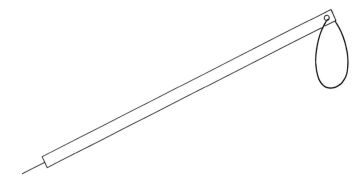

Fig. 4-18.   Push stick for table saw.

Hold stock securely with hands placed on the miter gauge and
    the stock. See Fig. 4-20.

Move the stock past the blade slowly.

Pull the board away from the blade before moving the miter
    gauge back to the original position.

To cut to length, cut the board slightly, pull it back to check
    location, and complete the cut.

Use an auxiliary board on the miter gauge for more support.
    See Fig. 4-21.

Many special cuts may be made on the table saw. Cuts that
require the use of the fence include cutting a rabbet with the grain,

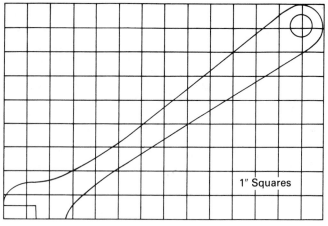

1″ Squares

Fig. 4-19.   Push stick for table saw made with ½″ pine stock.

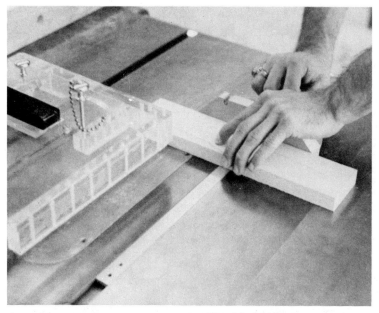

Fig. 4-20. Setup for crosscutting with a miter gauge.

a bevel, thin pieces, a cove, and a feather. Grooves for a spline may be cut in an edge, an end, in a flat miter, and in an edge miter. Cuts that require the miter gauge are dadoes and stop dadoes, tenons, miters, and cutting of duplicate parts.

In cutting a rabbet with the grain:

Select the appropriate blade and use the fence.

Cut the rabbet by making two cuts perpendicular to each other. See Fig. 4-22.

The first cut is the depth of the rabbet; the height of the blade is set for the width.

The second cut completes the joint. Set the distances from the blade to the fence to establish rabbet width. Saw height is the full depth.

This joint may also be cut with a dado head. If an auxiliary board is screwed to the fence, the dado head may be set for width and set next to the auxiliary board.

Grooves with the grain are also cut in this manner.

The bevel is cut by tilting the blade and using the fence as a

Fig. 4-21.   Auxiliary board used for crosscutting.

guide. Make a trial cut to see if the angle of tilt is accurate. Combine the trial pieces if certain combinations are desired. When accuracy is ensured, cut the good pieces.

Thin pieces may be cut by two easy methods. Narrow pieces of approximately an inch can be cut by ripping stock halfway through. Pull the piece back, turn end to end, and rip to meet the previous cut. This keeps the operator safe and eliminates the need to pass the push stick over the blade. Cutting narrow pieces, such as veneer 1/16-inch thick, is done on the outside of the blade. A board with parallel edges is needed. The fence is set to cut the good piece on the outside of the blade. Each cut requires a new setup.

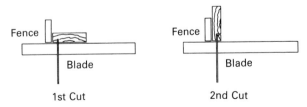

Fig. 4-22.   Cutting a rabbet with the grain.

A cove is cut by passing the workpiece across the blade at a slight angle:

Place the blade at the final height desired.

To determine the angle, use parallel rules. Allow to touch front and back of the blade. Rotate in a parallel manner until the distance between the rules is the desired width of the cove. See Fig. 4-23.

Clamp on a straightedge for a fence in front of the blade (side toward the operator). Leave the distance desired from the edge of the cove to the edge of the workpiece.

Lower the blade to only ⅛ inch above the table.

Move the workpiece along the fence. Make successively deeper cuts until the final depth is reached. See Fig. 4-24.

Move the workpiece steadily while holding against the fence. Do not pass your hands over the blade. Maintain the 4-inch margin of safety.

The feather cut is made in a miter joint by the use of a special

Fig. 4-23. Rotate parallel rules to determine width and angle of cove cut.

Fig. 4-24.   Cove cut after successive shallow cuts.

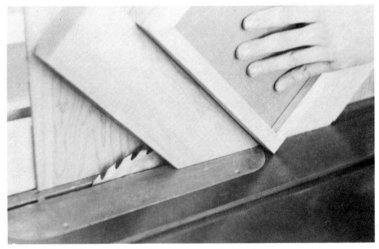

Fig. 4-25.   Fixture for cutting groove in feather.

fixture. See Fig. 4-25. The miter joints are first glued. The fixture holds the picture frame, door, or box structure so that the groove is cut across the miter joint. A dado head is usually used to cut a ¼-inch-wide groove.

Splines are also cut with the dado head. A spline on the edge of a piece is a normal ripping job, with the fence as a guide. When cutting the groove in the end of a board, a fixture holds the workpiece upright. See Fig. 4-26. This operation is done when making skeleton frames and frames for panel doors. The spline in a flat miter is carried out in a similar manner. The groove for the spline is cut with the help of a fixture. See Fig. 4-27. The spline in an edge miter is cut by tilting the blade perpendicular to the miter. The fence is used as a stop for the miter. Locate the cut so it is near the base of the miter and will not weaken the joint tip. Raise the blade to make the cut the desired depth. See Fig. 4-28.

Dadoes and grooves are cut with the dado head. The dado head consists of two outside cutters and inside chippers. The width depends upon the number of chippers used. The miter gauge is used as a guide.

Remove the blade and table insert.

Place the dado head on the arbor with the chippers evenly

Fig. 4-26. Fixture for cutting groove for spline.

Fig. 4-27. Fixture used to hold miter to cut groove for spline.

      spaced. Make sure the swagged teeth lie in the gullet of the outside teeth.

Place washer and nut, and tighten.

Use the insert with wide opening for dado cutting.

Dadoes are cut across the grain with the miter gauge.

Make a trial cut for width and depth. Paper washers may be used between the chippers to get slightly wider cuts.

Pass the work over the blade slowly to avoid chipping.

The auxiliary board on the miter gauge gives good support behind the cutter.

A blind dado is made by placing a stop block on the back of the table.

When the board reaches the stop block, turn off the machine and wait for the blade to stop before lifting the board.

      Tenons may also be cut with a dado head. A clearance block is used on the fence. This method makes a tenon with equal depth on all sides of the workpiece. See Fig. 4-29. The fence is used as a stop when the cut is not made all the way through.

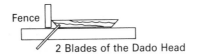

Fence

2 Blades of the Dado Head

Fig. 4-28.   Cutting a spline in an edge miter.

Miters may be cut with a combination or crosscut blade. The crosscut makes a smooth cut that looks good on the surface. A mitering fixture assures accurate miter joints at all times. See Fig. 4-30. Mating pieces are cut on the left and right of the fixture, which slides in the table saw slots.

Duplicate parts are crosscut by use of a clearance block on the fence. See Fig. 4-31. Make the measurement between the blade and the clearance block. Move the block to the front of the machine and clamp it to the fence. This supplies clearance so that when the pieces are cut off they do not pinch between the fence and the blade.

Fig. 4-29.   Tenon cut with a dado head.

Fig. 4-30.   Miter fixture used to cut accurate miters.

Jointer

The basic purpose of the jointer is to develop registration surfaces on the face and edge of stock before further machining is done. Since plywood and finished materials are used for many home projects, a small jointer is very useful for smoothing edges. See Fig. 4-32. When the edges are cut, a 1/16-inch allowance is left on for jointing smooth.

The jointer consists of infeed and outfeed tables, cutter head with three blades, fence, guard, and base. See Figs. 4-33 and 4-34. The infeed table is adjusted for depth of cut. For most jobs this is 1/16 inch. Wider and denser material will require a shallower cut. The outfeed table is adjusted to the height of the cutting circle of the blades. This receives the stock when the cut is complete. The fence provides vertical support for the material. It is normally at a right angle to the table, but can be tilted for chamfers and bevels. The guard protects the operator and swings aside when cutting is

Fig. 4-31. Setup for crosscutting duplicate parts with a clearance block.

being done. The size of a jointer is determined by the length of the blades, which determines the capacity of the machine. Jointers are available in various sizes from 4 inches up. See Fig. 4-35.

Consideration of the material is important when preparing to cut. The grain should be pointed back and down. To determine grain direction, look at the surface adjacent to the one being cut. Cutting with the grain will give a smooth cut. Always have a minimum of 10 inches of registration in contact with the table to avoid tipping and kickback. If you are cutting end grain, the board must be 10 inches wide. Place the concave surface down to get a registration surface. See Fig. 4-36. Do the large, flat surface first; all other surfaces will be squared with this one. Cut the edge square with the first surface. If the material has large warpage defects, cut it into smaller pieces to machine, still above the 10-inch minimum. Stock thinner than ½ inch should be sanded smooth.

To cut, place the material on the infeed table and advance slowly. As the board approaches the outfeed table, move the leading

Fig. 4-32.   Four-inch jointer and stand. *(Courtesy Delta International Machine Corporation)*

hand backward. Never run your hands through the area around the blades; keep at least a 4-inch margin of safety. Reach over to hold the piece down on the outfeed table, first with the left hand and then with the right. If boards are difficult to hold by hand or are

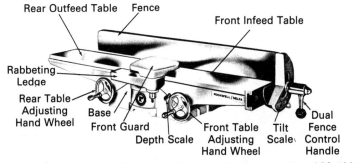

Rear Outfeed Table Fence

Front Infeed Table

Rabbeting Ledge

Rear Table Adjusting Hand Wheel

Base

Front Guard

Depth Scale

Front Table Adjusting Hand Wheel

Tilt Scale

Dual Fence Control Handle

Fig. 4-33.   Parts of a 6" jointer. *(Courtesy Delta International Machine Corporation)*

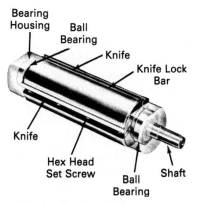

Bearing Housing

Ball Bearing

Knife

Knife Lock Bar

Knife

Hex Head Set Screw

Ball Bearing

Shaft

Fig. 4-34.   Parts of the cutter head.

Fig. 4-35.   Eight-inch long-bed jointer and stand. *(Courtesy Delta International Machine Corporation)*

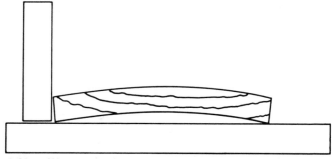

Fig. 4-36. Warpage defect down on the jointer to get a registration surface.

small, push sticks should be used. See Figs. 4-37 and 4-38. The flat push stick with handle is used when preparing surfaces. The narrow push stick is used on small pieces or when jointing an edge. Be sure to hold pieces down on the outfeed table to get a registration surface. If rough cuts occur, reverse the grain direction and try again. A slower feed may also help on some boards.

Edges of plywood may be jointed smooth. This is necessary after sawing to get a good gluing surface. These are needed for joints and where trim is applied. Cut in 1 inch on the edge, then turn the board around and do the remainder. See Fig. 4-39. When you reach the notch, pick up the piece. This prevents splitting the edge. The end grain of solid wood may also be jointed in this manner. The piece would need to be 10 inches wide to have good registration on the table. Keep surfaces against the fence to get a square corner.

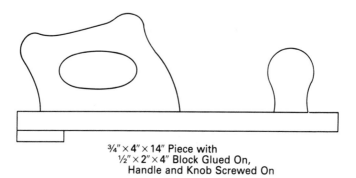

¾" × 4" × 14" Piece with
½" × 2" × 4" Block Glued On,
Handle and Knob Screwed On

Fig. 4-37. Push stick for jointing flat surfaces.

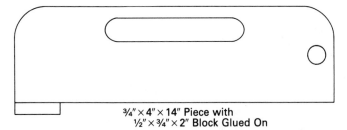

¾" × 4" × 14" Piece with
½" × ¾" × 2" Block Glued On

Fig. 4-38.   Push stick for jointing small pieces on edge.

Band Saw

The band saw is very convenient for many cabinetmaking jobs. See Fig. 4-40. Cutting is done with guides or freehand. This permits cutting curves in all thicknesses of stock, ripping and crosscutting in rough stock or finished pieces, and cutting circles and duplicate parts, among other jobs. Small projects and craft work are completed easily with the band saw.

The band saw consists of two large wheels and a continuous blade. See Fig. 4-41. The upper wheel is adjusted to align the blade. It is raised for proper tension and tilted to center the blade on the wheels. Blades are available in various widths, from ⅛ inch to 1½ inches. A blade for general use would be ¼ or ⅜ inch wide. The blade is held in position by the upper and lower guide assemblies. See Figs. 4-42 and 4-43. The guides should hold the blade in line. The ball-bearing support keeps the blade from moving backward.

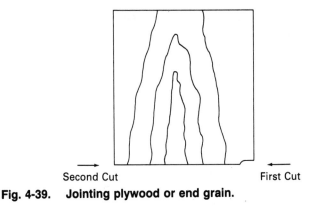

Second Cut   First Cut

Fig. 4-39.   Jointing plywood or end grain.

Fig. 4-40. Fourteen-inch band saw and stand. *(Courtesy Delta International Machine Corporation)*

When cutting, the guide post should be moved to place the upper guide within ¼ inch of the work.

Many cutting operations are done by following layout lines. Cut close to the line and allow enough material for future smoothing. To aid in cutting without pinching the blade, relief cuts may be made in the scrap stock. See Fig. 4-44. Nibble cuts will help to get into small corners. See Fig. 4-45. Back up and go forward several times to complete the cut. Tangent cuts are used where a curve is too tight for the blade size. See Fig. 4-46. Cut as tightly as the blade

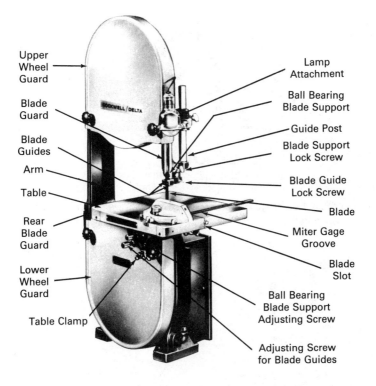

Fig. 4-41. Parts of a 14″ band saw. *(Courtesy Delta International Machine Corporation)*

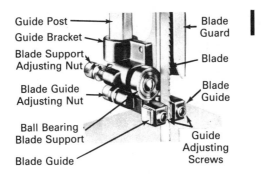

Fig. 4-42. Upper guide assembly. *(Courtesy Delta International Machine Corporation)*

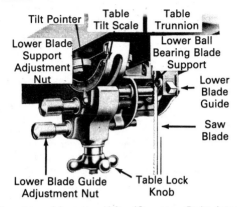

Fig. 4-43. **Lower guide assembly.** *(Courtesy Delta International Machine Corporation)*

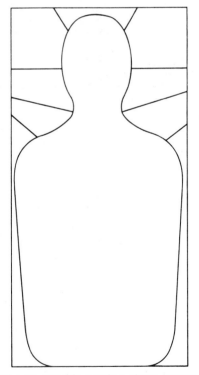

Fig. 4-44. **Relief cuts used in cutting sharp curves.**

Fig. 4-45.   Nibble cuts used in small areas.

allows, and continue on with that arc. Cut another tangent in the same way to take off more of the waste material.

Special techniques will also help in making various cuts. Lay out on the correct side of the material so that the piece will not hit the arm. Make short cuts first so you won't have to back out of the longer cut. Make straight cuts before curved ones. Drill turning holes in areas where a tight fit is anticipated.

Many special operations can be carried out on the band saw. Resawing is cutting stock on edge into thinner pieces. The operation is begun by cutting kerfs from both edges on the table saw. Consecutive deeper cuts will then allow the band saw to finish the cut easily. See Fig. 4-47. The entire job may be done on the band saw if you want to save material with the thinner saw blade.

Compound cutting is done when a shape is needed on all sides of a piece. The pattern is drawn on adjacent sides. Two opposite sides are cut. The waste stock may be put back in place and held with tape. See Fig. 4-48. This gives square registration surfaces for cutting the second half of the pattern.

Circles are cut by means of a circle-cutting jig. See Fig. 4-49. The jig extends to the right of the blade and provides a center for

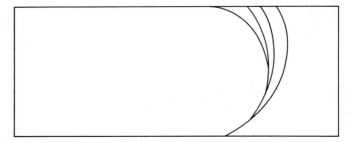

Fig. 4-46.   Tangent cuts used on a small radius.

Fig. 4-47. Resawing with table saw and band saw.

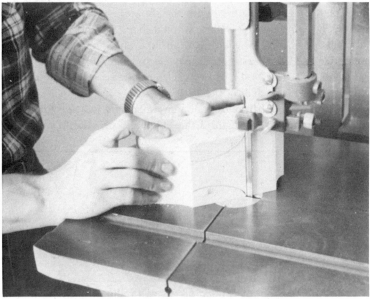

Fig. 4-48. Compound cuts with pieces taped together.

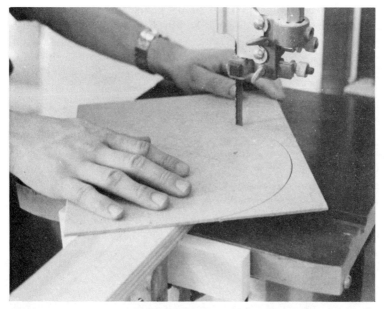

Fig. 4-49. Circles are easily cut with a circle-cutting jig.

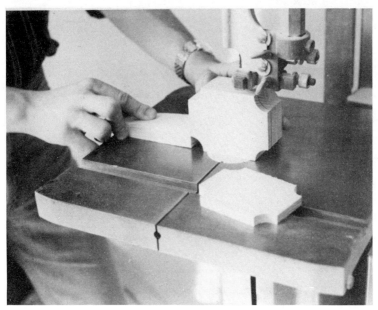

Fig. 4-50. Shapes recut for decorative trim with push stick.

the workpiece to pivot upon. A simple jig may be constructed with a board for a work surface and an attached cleat to clamp to the edge of the band saw table. A nail is driven in and the head cut off to provide a pivot point. Place the edge of the work against the blade. Lower the center onto the nail and begin turning to make the circle. The center in the workpiece may be predrilled to accept the nail. Use a sharp blade so that it will cut a true circle and not creep left or right.

Duplicate shapes are easily cut by using small brads in the waste stock to hold several pieces together. The parts are all cut at once by following a drawing on the surface. Parts may also be clamped and cut. This works well for large parts where clamps will be off the table and not interfere with cutting. Duplicate parts may also be cut by first cutting the shape in a thicker piece of stock and then resawing the block into thinner pieces. See Fig. 4-50.

CHAPTER 5

Portable Electric Tools

- **Electric Drill**
- **Circular Saw**
- **Saber Saw**
- **Router**
- **Sanders**

The home craftsman will find that a few portable electric tools will do most of the jobs required in many cabinetmaking projects and will duplicate the work done by larger, more expensive machines. With basic knowledge and some skill, fine results can be achieved. The portable tools will require much less space and a smaller initial investment. Various machines may be added to the workshop as you learn from experience what you need.

Working with portable tools will necessitate purchasing wood that is surfaced and of even thickness. This would include plywoods, standard pine materials, composition boards, and moldings. If hardwoods are used, they must be purchased in surfaced form. Projects in this book can be made with limited amounts of hardwoods. Most material will be available at a local lumber yard.

As you prepare to work with portable electric tools, become familiar with their use and care. Consult the manufacturer's specifications for the proper setup of the tool and follow their suggestions for the safe use of each tool. The following is a list of safety rules for all portable electric tools.

Have your safety glasses ready as you begin work.

Know the application and limitations of the tool.

Use the proper tool for the job.

Have the tool properly set up before plugging it in.

Remove adjusting keys and wrenches before turning on the power.

Do not jerk cords or use frayed cords or loose or broken plugs or switches.

Have tools properly grounded and be careful when working in damp locations or where combustibles are stored.

Have material properly supported before beginning to work.

Do not force the tool; this is dangerous, and it cuts poorly.

Keep cords out of the way of the blade and avoid tangling them under foot.

Disconnect tools when not in use.

Do not overreach; keep proper footing and balance at all times.

Use proper extension cords, heavy enough to carry the needed current. See Table 5-1.

Review additional safety rules for hand tools and machines; many of these will also apply to portable electric tools.

Table 5-1. Wire Gauge Number for Cord Length and Amperage Rating

Ampere Rating Range @115V	Length of Cord in Feet					
	25 ft.	50 ft.	100 ft.	200 ft.	300 ft.	400 ft.
3–4	18	18	16	12	10	10
4–5	18	18	14	12	10	8

Electric Drill

Electric drills are available in various sizes and horsepower ratings. Size relates to the shank diameter that the drill chuck can receive. Most common are ¼-, ⅜-, and ½-inch diameters. The larger chuck size is desirable for many cutting devices used. See Fig. 5-1.

Various types of drills are also available. See Fig. 5-2. The pistol

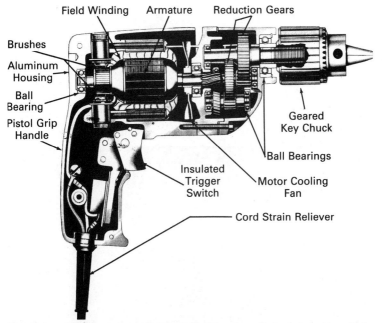

Fig. 5-1. Heavy-duty portable drill. *(Courtesy Delta International Machine Corporation)*

types are suitable for home use. The other types shown are large-capacity, heavy-duty drills for commercial use. Motors would be rated at 4 or more amps with gearing for power and torque.

Many options should be considered before purchasing drills for home use. A variable speed drill is very useful; it permits starting a hole without wandering. Slower speeds are also necessary for placing screws and for use with larger cutting tools, and are most effective with carbide tip bits. An adjusting knob for presetting maximum speed below normal maximum is available. This option allows continual use of lower selected speeds. A reversing switch is incorporated into the on-off switch. This is useful in taking out screws and backing out stuck bits. Many drills are now double insulated so that maximum protection is available without grounding.

There are also drills that can provide a hammer action for chiseling and drilling in concrete. Rechargeable models are also available, providing complete freedom from cords for special jobs.

A wide range of accessories is available for electric drills. In

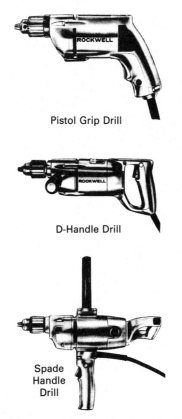

Pistol Grip Drill

D-Handle Drill

Spade
Handle
Drill

Fig. 5-2. Various types of drills. *(Courtesy Delta International Machine Corporation)*

addition to standard bits, there are various adjustable screw drills, larger bits, masonry drills, and hole saws for large holes. Included are wire wheels, grinding wheels, sanders, and buffers. Conversion tools allow use as a screwdriver of any type or a socket set. The electric drill is a much-used tool in the workshop.

Circular Saw

The portable circular saw does the work of both the radial arm saw and table saw. See Fig. 5-3. The saw is the most effective means of cutting large panels into smaller parts. See "Laying Out Rough

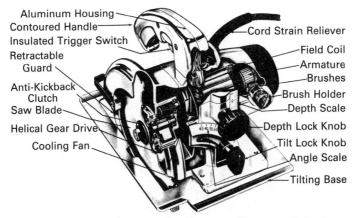

Aluminum Housing
Contoured Handle
Insulated Trigger Switch
Retractable
Guard
Anti-Kickback
Clutch
Saw Blade
Helical Gear Drive
Cooling Fan

Cord Strain Reliever
Field Coil
Armature
Brushes
Brush Holder
Depth Scale
Depth Lock Knob
Tilt Lock Knob
Angle Scale
Tilting Base

Fig. 5-3.   Parts of a portable circular saw. *(Courtesy Delta International Machine Corporation)*

Sizes" in Chapter 6. It is the best tool for cutting boards and dimension stock on the job for building construction.

The size of the saw is determined by the diameter of the blade. Most common is a 7-inch blade. This is a large-capacity machine. It can cut through a 2-by-4 at a 45-degree bevel. Many different types of saw are presently available, with varying capacities. See Fig. 5-4.

Blades are very similar to those used on the table saw and radial arm saw. Only the recommended blade size should be used on the saw, with the proper-size arbor hole. A large-toothed combination blade is most often used. See Fig. 5-5. This is a general-purpose blade for crosscutting and ripping where the finish of the cut is not critical. Many other blades are available, to be chosen according to the specific job being done and type of cut desired.

To change a blade, unplug the saw, retract the blade guard, and set the blade on a scrap piece of wood. Press down the saw to keep the blade from turning. Turn the clamping screw counterclockwise with the special wrench provided. Tap the wrench with a mallet if it is extremely tight. Take off the clamp screw, washer, and blade. Put on the new blade with the teeth pointing forward, making sure washers and screw are mounted properly. Tighten the clamp screw by hand and then with the wrench. Again press the blade teeth into a board to keep from turning.

Portable Saw
with
Built-in Brake

Worm Drive Saw
with
Blade on Left Side

Fig. 5-4. Types of circular saws. *(Courtesy Delta International Machine Corporation)*

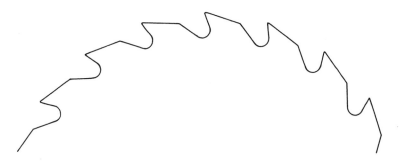

Fig. 5-5. Large-toothed combination blade.

When cutting, make sure the work is well supported and the saw is securely held. Place the good side of the material down, since the blade cuts upward. This will keep the face side from splitting. The saw may be directed either freehand, along a line, or used with a straightedge to ensure a straight cut. The base of the saw should be supported on the larger piece. It should not be supported by any piece that will fall away when the cut is made. See Fig. 5-6.

Advance the saw at a speed that cuts without the saw laboring. This speed will vary according to the thickness and density of the material, as well as the sharpness of the blade and the moisture content of material. If the saw begins to labor, slows down, or goes off the line, release the trigger and allow the blade to stop. Withdraw the saw, check the setup, and begin the cut again. Never force or twist the saw in the kerf. This will only cause problems.

Cuts made in the center of a piece are begun with the blade guard raised. Do this with the retracting lever on the guard. Start the saw with only the front of the base touching the work. See Fig. 5-7. Lower the saw to pierce the wood, and begin the cut.

To complete any cut, release the trigger and allow the blade to stop. Remove from the wood; the guard will automatically close. Never reach under the work. The blade is always exposed underneath while cutting.

Fig. 5-6.   Support the saw on a larger piece.

Fig. 5-7.   Beginning a cut in the center of the material.

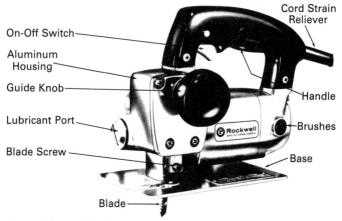

On-Off Switch

Aluminum Housing

Guide Knob

Lubricant Port

Blade Screw

Cord Strain Reliever

Handle

Brushes

Base

Blade

Fig. 5-8.   Heavy-duty bayonet saw. *(Courtesy Delta International Machine Corporation)*

Saber Saw

The saber saw, often called a bayonet saw or hand jigsaw, is one of the most useful in the shop. See Fig. 5-8. This portable saw will cut curves, do internal and external cutting, and cut to a straight edge. It will do the jobs of both the band saw and the jigsaw.

A great variety of blades are available for this saw. The blades will allow cutting of all types of wood, metal, and plastics. Various sizes and coarseness of blades can be selected for each job. Be sure that three teeth are in contact with the material at all times. Tighten the blade in the chuck securely before beginning to cut.

The various blades and saw types available make this an extremely versatile tool. See Fig 5-9. It can cut in any position—overhead, in corners, and in other hard-to-reach locations. The base can be tilted for bevel cuts. Variable-speed and two-speed models allow the selection of speeds to fit the material, faster speeds usually being used on softer materials. Blade action makes possible a plunge cut without first drilling a hole in the material. See Fig. 5-10.

When cutting, follow layout lines as closely as possible. Cutting is toward the base on the upward stroke. This necessitates laying out on the back side of some woods, such as paneling, to get a clean cut on the face side. Hold the material securely.

Heavy Duty
Bayonet Saw

Tiger
2-Speed All-Purpose Saw

Fig. 5-9.   Various types of saws. (*Courtesy Delta International Machine Corporation*)

Fig. 5-10. Making a plunge cut with a saber saw.

As you cut, it will be necessary to go past sharp corners, then come back and cut out the corner or confined area. See Fig. 5-11. This can be done with a series of nibble cuts to the corner. Do not force the saw, but hold it solidly and allow it to do the work.

Router

The router is used for making decorative cuts and joints in wood. It consists of a motor and base. See Fig. 5-12. The bit is held in the motor. The motor is raised up and down in the base to adjust for different cuts. Various motor sizes and styles of machine are available. See Fig. 5-13.

The most common bits are one-piece, two-fluted bits with and without a pilot. These are available in many shapes to make deco-

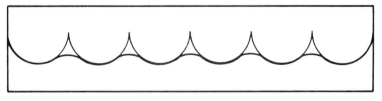

Fig. 5-11. Make first cut and return to trim corners.

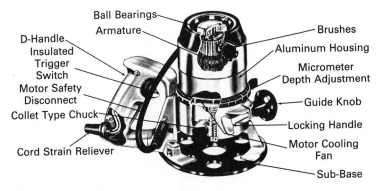

Ball Bearings

Armature

D-Handle

Insulated
Trigger
Switch

Motor Safety
Disconnect

Collet Type Chuck

Cord Strain Reliever

Brushes

Aluminum Housing

Micrometer
Depth Adjustment

Guide Knob

Locking Handle

Motor Cooling
Fan

Sub-Base

Fig. 5-12.   Router, 1¼ horsepower.

Fig. 5-13.   Router, 1½ horsepower. *(Courtesy Delta International Machine Corporation)*

rative cuts and as straight bits for cutting joints. See Fig. 5-14. Bits are also available with a threaded arbor. These bits allow use with or without a pilot. Pilots of various sizes can be used, and may be a ball-bearing type.

Place the bit in the collet chuck and tighten with the wrenches provided. Some machines allow the motor to be removed from the base for setup. Others have a locking device built in, and only one wrench is needed. Insert the bit at least ½ inch into the collet. Lower the motor to expose the bit the depth of cut desired. Lock the motor securely in the base.

The cutter of the router revolves in a clockwise direction. Cutting is best done moving from left to right, or counterclockwise, as

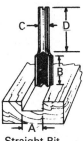

Straight Bit

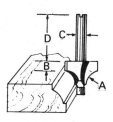

Beading Bit

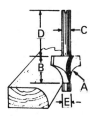

Rounding Over Bit

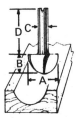

Core Box Bit

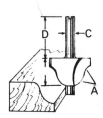

Roman Ogee Bit

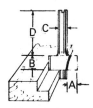

Rabbeting Bit

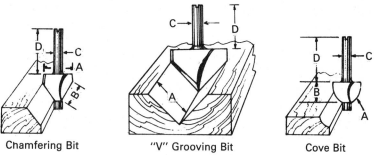

Chamfering Bit   "V" Grooving Bit   Cove Bit

Fig. 5-14. Common shapes of router bits.

you face the workpiece. It is often best to make several light cuts to reach the final depth desired. Feed at a speed that cuts efficiently. Going too slowly will cause the wood to burn, too fast will make a ragged cut.

Cutting with the router is directed by several methods. The pilot limits the depth of cut. It rides along the edge of the wood and restricts sideways movement to a given distance. The pilot may be a solid metal tip or a ball-bearing type. A router accessory called the edge guide can also be used. This guides along the work. See Fig. 5-15. A straightedge may be clamped to the work. The base of the router guides along the straightedge. This is most effective when cutting joints with a straight bit. See Fig. 5-16. A template may also be used to direct the router. A template guide is placed in the base of the router to follow the template, which permits you to cut interesting shapes and designs. Freehand routing may also be done without any guiding device. A pattern is usually drawn on the wood; the design or the background may then be cut away. Use a small bit and shallow cut when beginning this type of work.

Cuts on smaller workpieces are best made by mounting the

Fig. 5-15.   Router directed by an edge guide.

Fig. 5-16.   Joint cut directed by a straightedge.

router in a shaper table. See Fig. 5-17. A homemade shaper table is discussed in Chapter 7. The work may be directed by a fence, a straightedge, or the use of a pilot bit. The shaper table makes cutting on smaller parts much safer.

The router is an extremely useful tool in the home workshop. Many interesting operations and projects can be carried out with this tool, which has a number of accessories available for special projects.

Sanders

The portable belt sander may be used to smooth the surfaces of completed cabinets. See Fig. 5-18. This machine cuts down wood quickly, so great care must be taken. Only a small amount of work will do a great deal of cutting. The belt sander is available in various styles and sizes. See Fig. 5-19.

The size of the machine is determined by belt size. The belts are 3 or 4 inches wide and of various lengths. To install a new belt,

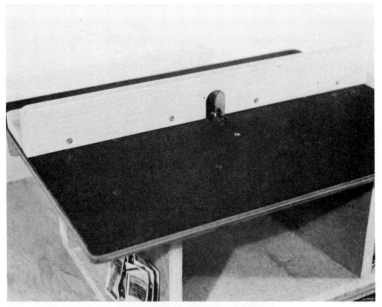

Fig. 5-17.   Router mounted in a shaper table.

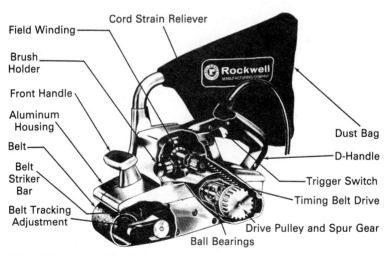

Fig. 5-18.   Dustless belt sander. *(Courtesy Delta International Machine Corporation)*

3 Inch × 24 Inch Belt Sander

4 Inch × 24 Inch Belt Sander

Fig. 5-19. Sizes of belt sanders. *(Courtesy Delta International Machine Corporation)*

release tension on the belt. Place a new belt on with the arrow on the inside pointing in the direction of rotation. Center on the pulleys by using the tracking adjustment provided.

Clamp the work securely. Hold the sander off the surface when turning it on. Lower it easily to the surface, with the rear touching first. Sand by moving the machine back and forth, and at the same time work from left to right. Keep the machine moving so it does not dig in, and do not allow it to sit with its full weight on the wood. Maintain control by moving and lifting.

End grain of solid wood may be sanded by holding the piece on end. Clamp additional boards flush on both sides to provide a wider surface for supporting the sander and keeping the end square and true. See Fig. 5-20. This develops a clean, beautiful end grain for table surfaces.

Fig. 5-20. Sanding end grain with a belt sander. *(Courtesy Delta International Machine Corporation)*

Finish sanding of cabinets may be done with a pad or finishing sanders. See Fig. 5-21. This sander is not a cure-all, and should also be used with care to prevent surfaces from getting out of square or worn down too far. Many types and sizes are available. See Fig. 5-22.

The size of the machine is determined by the size of abrasive sheet needed. Coarseness of abrasive should be selected according to the type of work being done. A standard 9-by-11-inch abrasive sheet is cut into three or four sheets for the machine. The abrasive is held in place by clips or a roller device turned with a screwdriver.

To use, hold the sander off the surface when turning it on. Set it evenly on the stock to sand. Apply a solid pressure and move back and forth, at the same time moving from side to side. Brush the dust aside and continue inspecting as you proceed.

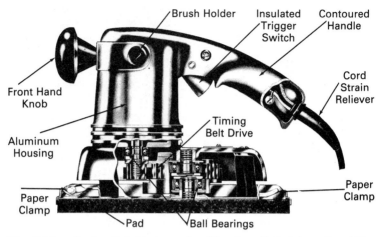

Brush Holder — Insulated Trigger Switch — Contoured Handle — Front Hand Knob — Cord Strain Reliever — Aluminum Housing — Timing Belt Drive — Paper Clamp — Paper Clamp — Pad — Ball Bearings

Fig. 5-21.   Pad or finishing sander. *(Courtesy Delta International Machine Corporation)*

Hi-Speed Sander

Dustless
Finishing Sander

Fig. 5-22.   Types of finishing sanders. *(Courtesy Delta International Machine Corporation)*

CHAPTER 6

Basic Construction

- Laying Out Rough Sizes
- Cutting to Rough Size
- Construction
- Gluing Up Stock
- Edge-to-Edge Gluing
- Clamping
- Face-to-Face Gluing
- Cutting to Finished Size
- Joints
- Joint Elements
- Types of Joints
- Joint Size

- Strengthening Joints
- Accuracy
- Glues
- Gluing and Clamping
- Tables
- Cabinets
- Plastic Laminates
- Doors
- Drawers
- Fasteners
- Preparing for Finishing
- Finishing

Laying Out Rough Sizes

Construction is begun by first laying out rough sizes on the material. This is done with ordinary layout and measuring tools. Mark with pencil or chalk. See Fig. 6-1. Large pieces will be laid out with the use of a framing square. See Fig. 6-2.

On solid wood, give consideration to material defects. The workpieces need to be made from clear stock; when using hardwoods, the knots, end checks, and other such defects should be cut out. In softwoods knots are not always a disadvantage and in many

Fig. 6-1. Lay out pieces with chalk or pencil.

Fig. 6-2. Lay out large pieces with a framing square.

projects look attractive. Cut out only loose knots, unsound wood, or other undesirable defects.

When laying out sheet stock, such as plywood, the arrangement of pieces is important for efficient use of the material. Allow the necessary extra stock between pieces for cutting and smoothing operations. See Fig. 6-3. If cutting is to be done with a saber saw or portable circular saw, lay out with the good side down to avoid splitting the good surface. Place the good side up when using a hand saw or table saw to avoid splitting. On all workpieces, be sure the grain runs the long direction of the piece.

Cutting to Rough Size

When cutting solid stock to rough size, a radial arm saw is good for crosscutting, a band saw for ripping. See Figs. 6-4 and 6-5. This can also be done with a hand saw, saber saw, or portable circular saw. Be sure that long pieces are well supported when cutting. See Fig. 6-6. Support so that the saw will not pinch when the cut is com-

Fig. 6-3. Lay out plywood parts with cutting space between lines.

Fig. 6-4. Crosscutting to rough size on the radial arm saw.

Fig. 6-5. Ripping to rough size on the band saw.

Fig. 6-6. Support long pieces with a roller device.

pleted. Develop the registration surfaces on the jointer and cut the individual workpieces to finished size. The table saw is good for finished crosscutting and ripping when a registration surface and edge can be used. You may also use hand tools.

When cutting sheet stock to rough size, a portable circular saw is most convenient. A hand saw or saber saw can be used. Most important is that the 4-by-8-foot sheet, or any other size, be well supported when the piece is cut off. When working alone, a good practice is to place the sawhorses perpendicular to the cut. See Fig. 6-7. The saw is set to protrude just below the surface, and so cuts the sawhorses only slightly. See Fig. 6-8. Long ripping cuts completely through the 8-foot length, are usually made first. The saw can be used freehand or with a straightedge. See Fig. 6-9. This can be clamped at each end or held in place with small nails.

Crosscutting of plywood can easily be done on a radial arm saw. The good side is placed up and a crosscut or other fine-toothed blade is used. Since the capacity of the saw may not be sufficient to complete the cut, it is necessary to follow layout lines and cut from each side. See Fig. 6-10. With some practice this technique will work extremely well. Use a straightedge when cutting with the portable circular saw, or follow layout lines freehand. See Fig. 6-11.

When crosscutting veneered plywood, always place the good side so that the veneered surface will not be chipped. On the cutting line you can place masking tape, which is then cut through and helps give a cleaner edge. If the veneered surface seems extremely brittle,

Fig. 6-7. Support plywood pieces with sawhorses perpendicular to the cut.

Fig. 6-8. Saw blade protrudes just below the surface.

the surface of the cutting line may be slightly dampened with water; this helps eliminate chipping by softening the wood. Use extreme care to dampen only slightly. This will raise the grain, and therefore in some situations may be an undesirable technique.

Fig. 6-9. Ripping with saw guided by a straight edge.

Fig. 6-10. Follow layout lines to crosscut from both edges on the radial arm saw.

Fig. 6-11.   Crosscutting freehand with a portable circular saw.

Construction

When constructing furniture it is desirable to incorporate the advantages of veneered plywood and solid wood. Plywood can be used for any large panels. With softwood or hardwood plywood, this provides a large stable workpiece. Hardwood-veneered plywood provides the additional advantage of beautiful matched veneers on the surface. The solid wood is then used for structural members, facing, legs, and other such parts. These may be shaped, carved, or sanded smooth.

Gluing Up Stock

Where the use of veneered plywood is not desired, solid stock will have to be glued up to form large surfaces. See Fig. 6-12. Edge-to-edge gluing is used for this process. If thick pieces are needed for legs, they will be glued face-to-face. See Fig. 6-13.

Fig. 6-12.   Solid wood used for the sides of a hope chest.

Fig. 6-13.   Large solid wood legs need glue up.

Edge-to-Edge Gluing

Considerable care must be taken to arrange boards to make up a large surface. Determine grain direction by looking at the edges, and mark on the faces. Arrange annual rings in opposite directions to minimize warpage. Mark the registration surfaces so that the boards will remain in the same order. See Fig. 6-14.

For this joint it is necessary to cut the edges of all boards square. This will make it possible to glue up one large registration surface. After the edges have been prepared on the jointer, stack and check for a flat registration surface. See Figs. 6-15 and 6-16. This is the only method to determine true flatness; holding the boards together or laying them flat on a bench does not give an accurate indication. After checking for flatness, look for light through the joint. Light through the center is acceptable and will make a good "spring joint," which ensures that the ends will be tightly glued. Light at the ends is not good for this joint. See Fig. 6-17 (p. 181). To make a spring joint when using the jointer, push harder in the middle and feed the board much more slowly.

Clamping

When the pieces stack straight up and down and show the correct light, clamping may proceed. Use bar clamps with white glue. Place clamps on a bench or sawhorses so that they are ready for use. Place

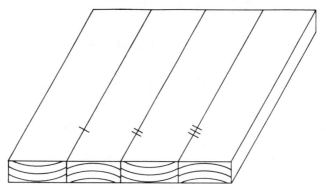

Fig. 6-14. **Annual rings in opposite directions to minimize warpage.**

Fig. 6-15.   Boards stacked on edge with warp.

boards in the clamps with the registration surface down and in order. Spread a thin coat of glue on all edges. Clamps should alternate on opposite sides to hold the pieces flat. Clamp gradually until each is secure. Boards are used to protect edges and distribute pressure. See Fig. 6-18. Do not tighten too securely; one hand pressure is sufficient. Look for slight squeeze-out as an indication of a good joint.

To ensure that the boards are down flat on the clamps, it may be necessary to tap with a mallet while clamping. To ensure they stay flat, clamp cleats on at each end. See Fig. 6-19. Place paper

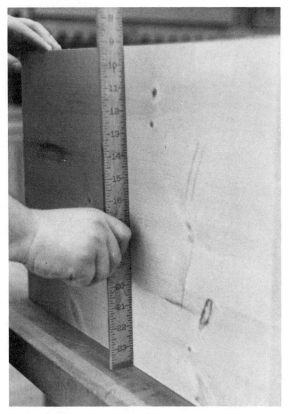

Fig. 6-16.   Boards stacked flat will produce a registration surface.

at the glue lines. Excess glue may be lifted off with a blade and the area washed to eliminate any trace of the glue. Wipe dry so the glue line is not affected.

Face-to-Face Gluing

Parallel clamps or small bar clamps may be used for face-to-face gluing. Joint boards to a registration surface. Spread a thin coat of glue on both surfaces, and clamp. See Fig. 6-20. Look for slight squeeze-out all the way around the joint. Make sure clamps are parallel, and readjust to ensure a good joint. See Fig. 6-21.

Ends Open, Not Acceptable

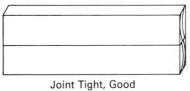

Joint Tight, Good

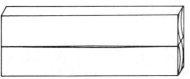

Spring Joint, Best

Fig. 6-17. Edge-to-edge spring joint.

Fig. 6-18. Alternate clamps with registration surface down.

Fig. 6-19. Install clamp boards to keep piece flat.

Fig. 6-20. Face-to-face gluing of legs.

Fig. 6-21. Readjust clamps if they are not parallel.

Cutting to Finished Size

Cutting to finished size is done according to the dimensions on the material bill. Up to this point parts have been rough cut from solid wood or plywood. In some cases larger pieces of solid stock have been glued up in preparation for this step.

On solid wood pieces the first step is to develop a registration surface. This is a flat and true surface from which all other surfaces can be squared; this is done on the jointer. After the surface is flat, the edge is made square with it. The second surface is then made parallel to the first. The second edge is ripped parallel and smoothed on the jointer. The ends are then cut square with the previous surfaces.

On plywood and other large pieces a registration edge is made straight and true on the jointer. This edge may be the factory edge, which will be straight. Always joint from both ends toward the center to avoid chipping (see the next section on the jointer). The second edge is then ripped parallel and smoothed on the jointer, and the ends are cut square with the previous edges. On plywood allow at least ⅟16 inch on each edge for jointing smooth.

Joints

After a workpiece has been properly squared up and is the desired size, the joints are cut. This must be done before registration surfaces are cut away. See Fig. 6-22. Square and true surfaces are needed for layout and for guiding pieces as joints are cut. Cutting shapes that involve cutting away registration surfaces is one of the last operations done before assembling and adding decorative trim.

The successful completion of joints involves many steps. The elements of good joint construction are listed and discussed below. For good results, all of them must be understood.

Fig. 6-22.   Cut joints before cutting away registration surface.

Joint Elements

Proper type of joint for the job.
Proper size of joint to fit the job.
Proper means of strengthening the joints.
Accuracy in layout and cutting.
Use of appropriate glues and techniques of gluing.
Proper clamping.

Types of Joints

When building any structure it is necessary to choose the appropriate joints. The need for strength, for good appearance, and for speed and ease of construction must all be considered. Strength is important for items such as tables or bookcases. Good appearance is important for picture frames or trim work. Speed and ease of construction become important in home building. Each project and situation will dictate the appropriate type of joint. These may be very simple or extremely complicated combinations of joints. In any case, a joint may be classified as one of seven basic types: butt, rabbet, dado, lap, miter, mortise and tenon, and finger or dovetail.

Butt Joints

The butt joint is a very simple and easy joint to make. The parts of a structure are placed in proper alignment and held with glue or fasteners. This is the common method of construction for a very simple box structure or for home building. Additional means of strengthening the joint is always necessary.

Three basic types of butt joint are generally used. See Fig. 6-23. The edge butt is typically used in making simple boxes, such as a toolbox, child's sandbox, and other such structures. The flat butt is typical of that used in making a separate facing structure for a cabinet. The edge-to-edge butt joint is used in developing wide surfaces from smaller boards. The edge-to-edge spring joint has been discussed in preparation of stock.

Rabbet Joints

The rabbet joint is very easy to make and is stronger than the butt joint. It is made by cutting a notch on the edge of one piece to

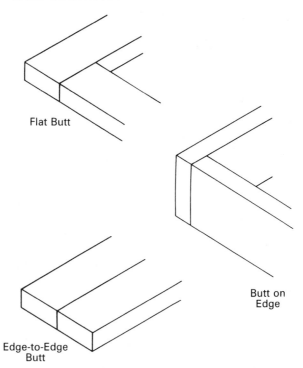

Flat Butt

Butt on Edge

Edge-to-Edge Butt

Fig. 6-23.   Basic types of butt joints.

receive the other. This is the common method of construction for box structures. Rabbet joints are glued and clamped or glued and fastened for assembly.

The rabbet joint is made on either the edge or the end of a workpiece. See Fig. 6-24. When cut on the end of a workpiece, the upright members will form a box. This is a typical method of making storage boxes, toolboxes, and drawers. When the rabbet is cut on the long edge of a workpiece, a panel is usually inserted. This may be the bottom of a box or the panel of a door.

Dado-Groove Joints

The dado-groove joint is a three-sided joint cut in from the edge of a workpiece. It provides good strength and is typically used in many cabinetmaking applications. When assembled with glue, the joint is extremely strong.

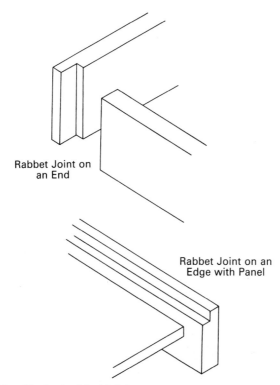

Rabbet Joint on
an End

Rabbet Joint on an
Edge with Panel

Fig. 6-24.   Typical rabbet joints.

The joint is made either across or with the grain. See Fig. 6-25. When made across the grain, it is referred to as a dado. This joint is used in case construction to insert a shelf or structural member of a cabinet. When the joint is made with the grain, it is called a groove. The groove is used to place the bottom of a toolbox or a door panel. When a clean appearance is desired, the joint may be made blind by stopping the cut short of the edge of a workpiece.

Lap Joints

In making a lap joint, equal amounts of material are taken from each piece. When the parts are assembled the surfaces are flush. Lap joints are often used to replace other joints where considerable strength is needed. The large glue surface makes the joint very strong.

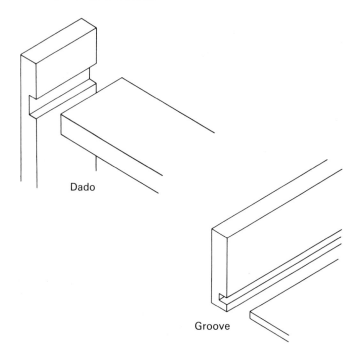

Fig. 6-25. Dado-groove joints.

Several types of lap joints are commonly used. See Fig. 6-26. The cross-lap can be made with pieces either flat or on edge. This permits an open structure such as a decorative grillwork, a framework for hanging plants, or a trellis. The end lap may be used to make a strong frame or door structure.

Miter Joints

A miter joint is a joint cut at any angle other than 90 degrees. The common miter joint is 45 degrees. See Fig. 6-27. Four corners then make up a square. Miters may be cut to form a pentagon, a hexagon, or other such many-sided structure. The advantage of the miter joint is its attractive appearance.

A miter joint needs to be reinforced. The end grain joint does not hold well because it is porous. Many devices may be used to strengthen the joint, from metal fasteners to wood inserts. Methods of strengthening joints are discussed below.

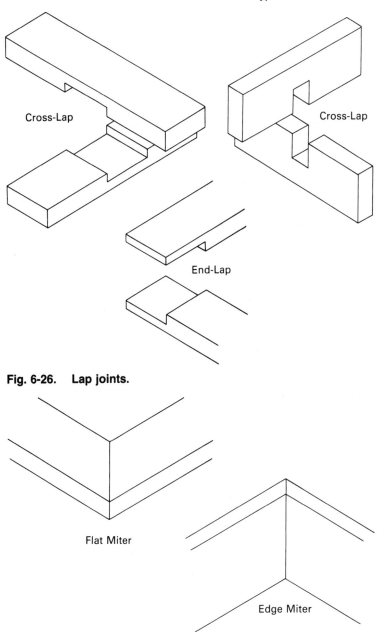

Fig. 6-26.   Lap joints.

Fig. 6-27.   Miter joints.

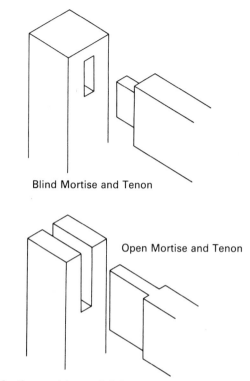

Blind Mortise and Tenon

Open Mortise and Tenon

Fig. 6-28.   Mortise and tenon joints.

Mortise and Tenon

In the mortise and tenon, the tenon is inserted into the mortise, making it one of the strongest woodworking joints. The large glue surfaces give the joint additional strength. Besides being strong, the joint also looks good.

Various types of mortise and tenon joint are made for various purposes. See Fig. 6-28. The open mortise and tenon can be used to lock together a frame, or sanded smooth to add to the appearance of a modern coffee table or end table. The blind mortise and tenon provides strength for common leg and rail structures. When constructing this joint the mortise is always made first so that the tenon can be carefully fitted to it.

Finger and Dovetail Joints

This category of joint includes those that are capable of locking together without additional means. See Fig. 6-29. These joints are exceptionally strong. They also enhance the appearance of the project.

The finger or box joint is used on various box structures, such as storage and shipping boxes or a collection box. To make this joint a special setup is needed on the table saw. Great skill is required to cut it by hand.

The dovetail joint comes in many varieties. Single large dovetails are used in the structure of some furniture pieces. The dovetail joints used in making drawers are cut with a router and dovetail jig. Great skill is also needed to cut multiple dovetails by hand.

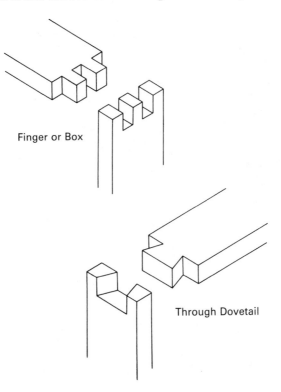

Finger or Box

Through Dovetail

Fig. 6-29.   Finger and dovetail joints.

Joint Size

The size of the wood joint is determined by the thickness of the material used, which will depend upon the standard sizes available and the basic requirements of the project being built. The thicker the stock, the larger the joint. In many situations the normal procedure would be to cut the joint halfway through the wood piece. This is the case with the dado, rabbet, and lap. Maximum strength needs to be developed without weakening any part of the joint.

Strengthening Joints

Many joints need to be strengthened with extra devices besides gluing. Any joint that involves the attachment of end grain needs to be reinforced. End grain does not hold well because it is porous. Common methods are metal fasteners, such as screws, nails, and special fasteners. Various other methods include wooden parts that are inserted and glued in place.

The most common device is the dowel. A dowel rod or commercial dowel pin may be used. See Fig. 6-30. Note that the pin has serrations to help in glue distribution and holding. The dowel is used for strengthening and alignment of joints. See Fig. 6-31. When a dowel is used, the joint is referred to by both names, e.g., a doweled butt joint or doweled miter joint.

To drill matching holes on joint parts, layout lines are first placed on the wood. See Fig. 6-32. Several types of commercial dowel jig are available; here a homemade device has been substi-

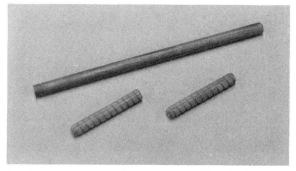

Fig. 6-30.   Dowel pins and dowel rod used for fasteners.

Fig. 6-31.   Dowel used for alignment and strength.

Fig. 6-32.   Layout lines on surface of joint.

tuted. See Fig. 6-33. The device is held in place by a parallel clamp and used on the end and edge of facing pieces. See Figs. 6-34 and 6-35.

A second method for locating matching holes is with dowel

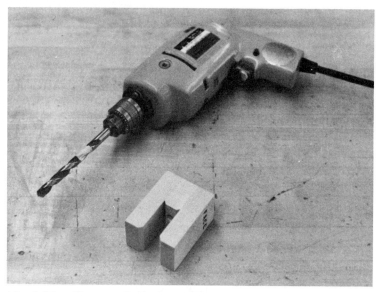

Fig. 6-33.   Homemade jig for drilling dowel holes.

Fig. 6-34.   Dowel jig used to drill end.

Fig. 6-35.   Dowel jig on edge, face of material the same direction.

centers. See Fig. 6-36. The first hole is drilled and the dowel center placed in it to mark the second piece. Dowel centers are available from many craft suppliers in several standard sizes.

An easy substitute for dowel centers is a nail. Place a small nail where the first hole will be. See Fig. 6-37. Cut off the head and use to mark the second piece. Owing to rotation of the bit and the wood grain, dowel holes will not always align perfectly. When this happens, glue a piece of dowel in one hole, cut flush, and redrill.

A spline is a very simple means of aligning and strengthening parts. The spline is a thin piece of wood placed in a groove in both parts of the joint. See Fig. 6-38. The spline can be made from plywood or hardboard. If solid wood is used, the grain should be perpendicular to the face of the joint. The groove for the spline is parallel to the length of the joint. See Figs. 6-39 and 6-40.

A feather is often used to strengthen a miter joint. See Fig. 6-41 (p. 198). The groove is cut perpendicular to the length of the joint. After gluing, the groove is cut on the table saw with a special fixture. See Fig. 6-42. The feather is inserted with the grain across the joint. See Fig. 6-43 (p. 199). The feather is a very attractive

Fig. 6-36. Dowel center used to locate matching holes.

Fig. 6-37. Cut-off nail used to locate matching holes.

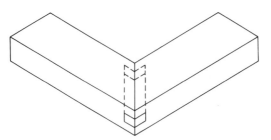

Fig. 6-38.   Spline in a miter joint.

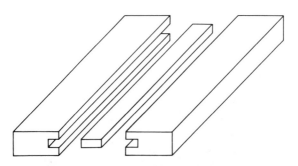

Fig. 6-39.   Hardboard or plywood spline in an edge-to-edge joint.

Fig. 6-40.   Hardboard spline in a skeleton frame.

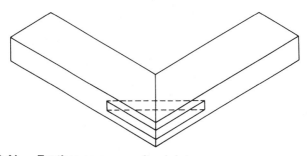

Fig. 6-41.   Feather across a miter joint.

Fig. 6-42.   Feather cut after joint is cut and glued.

fastener and greatly enhances the project design. See Fig. 6-44.

A joint may also be held with a wooden pin. A tapered or square pin may be used in the end of a through mortise. A round tapered pin is often used to lock a large mortise and tenon. A dowel may also be placed through a joint to lock parts together.

Glue blocks are often used to strengthen adjacent parts. These are made in triangle or square shapes. See Fig. 6-45. They should be held or clamped secure until the glue has begun to set.

Corner blocks are large pieces used to hold a table or chair frame. See Fig. 6-46. Great rigidity is added to the structure when they are glued and screwed in place. Be sure the grain runs the length of the piece.

The cleat is a specially made glue block. See Fig. 6-47. It is a square glue block with screws positioned to hold adjacent parts. See Fig. 6-48. The screw holes are drilled before assembly. The cleat aids in assembly and alignment. Great strength is achieved with the glue and screws.

Fig. 6-43.   Feather glued in place.

Fig. 6-44.   Resulting attractive feather joint.

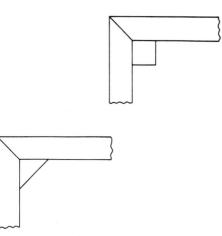

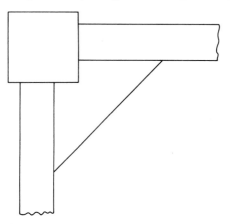

Fig. 6-45.   Triangle and square glue blocks glued in place.

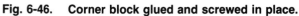

Fig. 6-46.   Corner block glued and screwed in place.

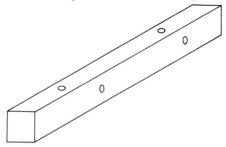

Fig. 6-47.   Square cleat drilled for screws.

Fig. 6-48. Cleat with screws holding adjacent parts.

Accuracy

When beginning actual work on a joint, accurate layout is essential. Use a sharp pencil or knife. Double-check the layout when it is completed. Be sure that you are working with left and right pairs when needed. Lay out on the correct side of plywood so that cutting tools will not chip the veneer on the good surface.

The cutting of joints needs to be done accurately, whether with hand tools or machines. Be sure tools are held square or in line with the layout. If necessary, guide saws and chisels with a guide block or jig. Be sure machines are cutting square and true. Make trial cuts before working on your good pieces, practicing on pieces that can be thrown away. Use sharp cutting edges and feed slowly enough so that the cuts are smooth. When the joints are completed the parts should slip together squarely and easily. A joint should not be filed or sanded.

Glues

Proper glue selection is extremely important. The product's ultimate use is the determining factor. For use out of doors a waterproof glue is needed. A second factor in glue selection is the time required for assembly. A product with several parts to be assembled will need a slow-drying glue.

Many types of glue are available at the local hardware store, often with a wide range of applications. Cabinetmakers can be guided by their specific task. For use with wood, only a few specific glues need to be considered.

Polyvinyl white glue is one of the best for woodworking. It comes ready to use in squeeze bottles and is relatively inexpensive. It is a quick-setting glue, but not waterproof. Since it dries quickly, clamps must be ready to place. Most joints will set within an hour. Elmer's White glue is an example of this type.

Aliphatic glues are a relatively new type of liquid glue that come ready to use in squeeze bottles. This yellow glue is primarily for woodworking and is heat and moisture resistant. It dries even more quickly than the white glues. Most joints may be removed from clamps in 30 minutes. Elmer's Professional Carpenter's glue is an example of this type.

Plastic resin glue comes as a brown powder that must be mixed with water. It is moisture resistant and can be used on projects intended for use out of doors. Since it does not set quickly, the woodworker has time to work on a structure and position and clamp the pieces, which is an important advantage in many assembly operations. This glue must be clamped overnight, or for at least 16 hours.

Resorcinol resin glue comes as a powder and liquid resin that must be mixed for use. The main advantage of this glue is that it is completely waterproof; it is used in boat building and other applications where there is extreme dampness. It is not often used for furniture and cabinetmaking because of the expense and the dark glue line that results. This glue must also remain clamped for 16 hours.

For most jobs the woodworker will need to use either the white glue or plastic resin glue. Properly used, they will make a joint that is extremely strong.

Gluing and Clamping

Gluing and clamping involves many steps, which are listed below.

Make sure joints have been properly cut.

Surfaces to be glued must be clean and dry.

Select all clamps that will be needed.

Make a trial run with all clamps and clamp boards in place.

The trial run will determine if the parts are the proper size and the project is square.

Use clamp boards to distribute pressure and protect exposed surfaces.

Select appropriate glue for the project.

Apply glue to both surfaces of the joints.

On end grain, allow the first coat to become tacky, and apply a second coat. Make sure all surfaces remain wet.

Clamp properly and apply pressure with one hand. Great pressure with two hands will create a starved joint or distort the wood.

Look for slight glue squeeze-out as an indicator of a good joint.

Again check for squareness.

Remove excess glue with a scraper and wash clean with a damp cloth. See Figs. 6-49 and 6-50.

Fig. 6-49.   Bar clamps parallel to shelves determine squareness.

Fig. 6-50.   Clamp boards distribute pressure and protect surfaces.

Tables

A table is a simple, open structure, consisting basically of legs, rails, and a top. See Fig. 6-51. Any table being built should be considered as such a structure. This will make it much easier for the builder to plan and organize his ideas. See Figs. 6-52 and 6-53.

The category of tables includes coffee tables, end tables, occasional tables, dining tables, and drawing tables. These may be more or less complicated to plan and build, but each is only a variation of the basic table.

A table of modern design would incorporate straight or simple

Fig. 6-51.   Basic coffee table with tapered legs.

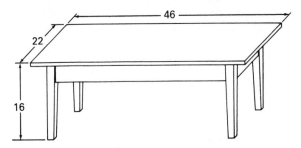

Fig. 6-52.   Coffee table dimensions.

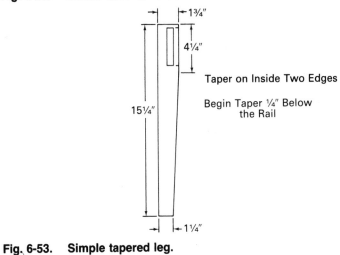

Taper on Inside Two Edges

Begin Taper ¼″ Below
the Rail

Fig. 6-53.   Simple tapered leg.

tapered legs. See Fig. 6-54. Various crossmembers or braces may be added to strengthen the legs. See Figs. 6-55 and 6-56. The complexity of the design will determine the joints and construction details.

Early American tables feature turned legs, which may be attached straight or at a slant. Rails often surround the base or cross to adjacent legs. See Fig. 6-57. Less expensive tables will have no rails to strengthen the legs, which are simply attached to the top with leg brackets and bolts.

Drafting tables involve the construction of leg structures as independent parts. The rails are normally in the center to allow for work room. These may be bolted in place to permit easy breakdown. Tops are made to tilt for efficient work. See Fig. 6-58.

Construction methods are generally the same for all tables. Attention is first paid to attaching the legs to the rails. This can be done with dowels, mortise and tenon joints, metal corner brackets, wooden corner blocks, or a combination of these. The method used

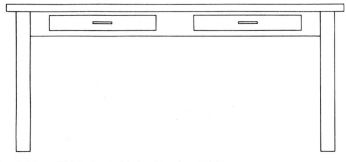

Fig. 6-54.   Thirty-inch-high planning table.

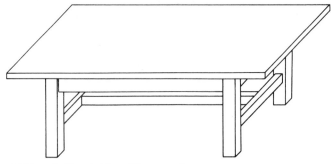

Fig. 6-55.   Coffee table with cross braces.

Fig. 6-56. Modern coffee table with additional crossmember.

Fig. 6-57. Early American coffee table with lower rails.

will be determined by the tools available and the type of wear the table will be subjected to when in use.

The mortise and tenon is an extremely strong joint for this purpose. See Fig. 6-59. In the absence of tools to cut this joint,

Fig. 6-58.   Center rails form skeleton of drafting table.

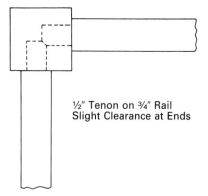

½″ Tenon on ¾″ Rail
Slight Clearance at Ends

Fig. 6-59.   Mortise and tenon joint.

dowels provide a good method. See Fig. 6-60. The wooden corner block can be used either alone or as a way of strengthening these joints. See Fig. 6-61. The wooden corner block and metal corner bracket may be used when you want removable legs. See Fig. 6-62.

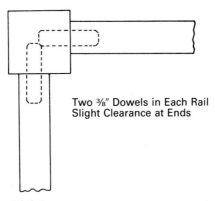

Two ⅜″ Dowels in Each Rail
Slight Clearance at Ends

Fig. 6-60. Dowel joint.

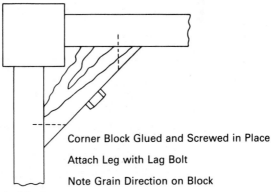

Corner Block Glued and Screwed in Place

Attach Leg with Lag Bolt

Note Grain Direction on Block

Fig. 6-61. Corner block.

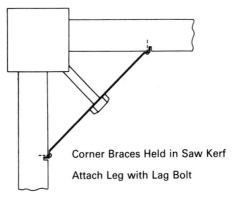

Corner Braces Held in Saw Kerf

Attach Leg with Lag Bolt

Fig. 6-62. Metal corner braces.

A simple method of constructing a rail structure is illustrated in Fig. 6-63. First, attach with screws four rails at the corners to form a box. Second, attach full corner blocks with glue and screws at each corner. Third, cut out each corner notch for the leg and drill for a lag bolt. Fourth, insert leg with glue and lag bolt.

Tops of tables are best if made of plywood. Hardwood plywood presents a stable, attractive surface with matched grain. To finish off the plywood edges, several different methods may be used: veneer or veneer tape, solid wood, shaped trim, or a drop edge. See Fig. 6-64. The various edge treatments finish to match the plywood

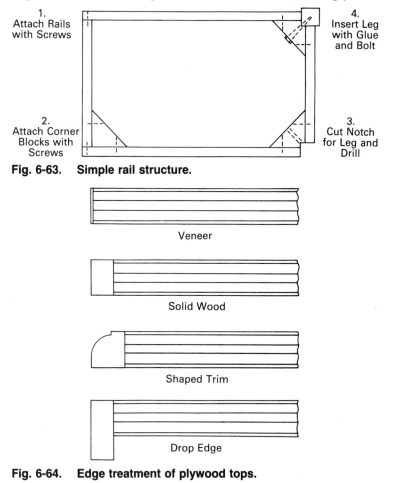

1.
Attach Rails
with Screws

4.
Insert Leg
with Glue
and Bolt

2.
Attach Corner
Blocks with
Screws

3.
Cut Notch
for Leg and
Drill

Fig. 6-63.   Simple rail structure.

Veneer

Solid Wood

Shaped Trim

Drop Edge

Fig. 6-64.   Edge treatment of plywood tops.

used. When softwood plywood is used for tops, it is usually covered with various composition materials, and edges are covered in a similar manner. See Fig. 6-65.

Tabletops may be attached by several means. Commercially made tabletop fasteners may be used. The round mortise type is placed on the rail of the table. A ¾-inch bit is used to drill a depression off-center of the rail. See Fig. 6-66. Hold with a screw in the rail and the tabletop. The square top fastener is placed in a saw kerf along the inside of the rail. Cut the kerf down ⅜ inch from the edge of the rail. Hold fastener to top with a round-head screw. See Fig. 6-67.

Various devices made in the shop can be used to fasten tops. Cleats are usually the primary choice. See Fig. 6-68. These are square pieces of wood drilled with matching holes. They are glued and screwed permanently to the rails. Screws hold the top in place.

Fig. 6-65.   Plastic laminate on edges of tabletop.

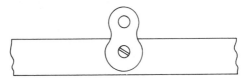

Fig. 6-66.   Top fastener set into drilled recess.

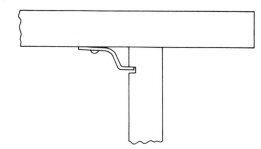

Fig. 6-67.   Top fastener held in saw kerf.

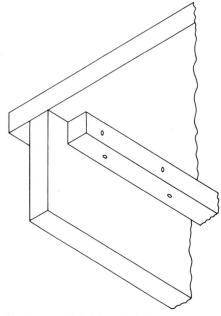

Fig. 6-68.   Cleat on underside of table.

Cabinets

Often the project the woodworker chooses to make is some type of cabinet. It may be an open structure, such as a bookcase, built-in shelves, or modular shelving units. See Figs. 6-69 and 6-70. Others are closed cabinets with doors and drawers. These include such items as chests, dressers, bedside tables, stereo cabinets, and wall cabinets. See Figs. 6-71 and 6-72.

Fig. 6-69. Living room bookcase.

Fig. 6-70. Built-in bookcase.

Fig. 6-71.   Desk from wall furniture arrangement.

Fig. 6-72.   Chest from wall furniture arrangement.

This type of cabinet is usually referred to as case goods. It is made with four sides and a back. As the cabinet is built, various methods may be used to make the sides, top, bottom, and back, including the use of solid wood, plywood, and frame and panel construction. Each project should be considered as basically a box.

As the cabinet is constructed, the sides are made first. The type of cabinet and furniture style will dictate how they will be made. Means of attaching the crossmembers are then constructed, some of which may require joints, such as dado, rabbet, or dowel. See Fig. 6-73. These joints may be covered with a narrow facing or made blind so they do not show on the front. In other situations, as when a wider facing will eventually hide the cleats, a simple cleat may be used to attach crossmembers. See Fig. 6-74.

When the basic box is completed, decorative trim and finish pieces are added. Several methods may be used to cover the edges and crossmembers of the box. Thin veneer edges may be applied with glue, or commercial banding may be purchased that is attached with contact cement. See Fig. 6-75. Solid wood trim pieces are the most desirable. Quarter-inch-thick facing may be glued and nailed. See Fig. 6-76. Thicker facing should be glued and clamped. Thickness varies depending upon future treatment, such as routing. See Fig. 6-77. Miter joints or butt joints are used at the corners. In some cases doweled facing of 1½-inch-wide boards is nailed in place

Fig. 6-73.   Start of a cabinet with skeleton frames in joints.

Fig. 6-74.   Start of cabinet with cleats.

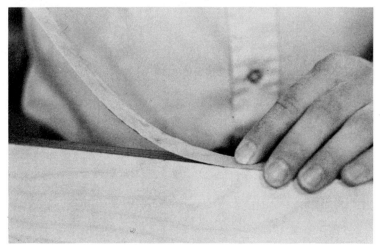

Fig. 6-75.   Use of commercial banding to trim plywood.

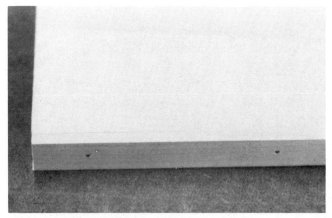

Fig. 6-76.   Solid wood facing glued and nailed.

Fig. 6-77.   Wider facing to allow for routing.

to cover the entire cabinet front. This allows for door and drawer openings. See Fig. 6-78.

One of the easiest cabinets to make is the kitchen cabinet or bathroom vanity, which can be made with plywood for sides of the box. See Table 6-1 (p. 219). Cut partitions and make a ⅜-by-¼-inch rabbet along the edge of the sides to receive the back. Cut the notch for the toeboard. Note layout measurements in Chapter 8. The notch

Fig. 6-78.   Doweled facing attached with glue and nails.

on the end partition allows the toeboard to be covered and facing to hang 1½ inches below the shelf. The center partition is made so that the toeboard can extend through, 4¼ inches high. Attach cleats in locations to hold crossmembers. Be sure to make partitions in pairs with the good side out.

Cut all notches with a saber saw or band saw. Cut cleats and attach with glue and nails. The base cleat is set back ¾ inch on the sides to receive the toeboard. See Fig. 6-79.

Begin assembly by gluing and nailing the shelf in place. Glue and screw crossmembers in place to strengthen the partitions. Be sure the box is square as this step is carried out. Install the toeboard. See Fig. 6-80.

Table 6-1. Kitchen Cabinet Material List

Dimensions are finished sizes.

Case		
Partitions	2 pc. ¾″ × 23¼″ × 34½″	Fir plywood
Base cleats	2 pc. ¾″ × 4¼″ × 20″	Fir plywood
Upper cleats	4 pc. ¾″ × 1½″ × 23″	Pine
Shelf	1 pc. ¾″ × 23″ × 16½″	Fir plywood
Crossmembers	4 pc. ¾″ × 1½″ × 16½″	Pine
Toeboard	1 pc. ¾″ × 4¼″ × 16½″	Fir plywood
Back panel	1 pc. ¼″ × 17¼″ × 30″	Fir plywood
Top		
Board	2 pc. ¾″ × 18″ × 25″	Fir plywood
Backsplash	1 pc. ¾″ × 4″ × 18″	Fir plywood
Covering	1 pc. 36″ × 2′	Formica
Screws	3 pc. 2¼″ #8 flat head	
	4 pc. 2″ #8 flat head	
Facing		
Horizontal	3 pc. ¾″ × 1½″ × 15″	Pine
Vertical	2 pc. ¾″ × 1½″ × 31″	Pine
Drawer Runners		
Horizontal	4 pc. ¾″ × 1¼″ × 23″	Pine
Screws	12 pc. 1¼″ #8 flat head	
Drawer		
Sides	2 pc. ¾″ × 5″ × 22″	Pine
Front, back	2 pc. ¾″ × 5″ × 13″	Pine
Front trim	1 pc. ¾″ × 6″ × 16″	Birch plywood
Bottom	1 pc. ¼″ × 13″ × 21¼″	Fir plywood
Door		
Front	1 pc. ¾″ × 16″ × 21¾″	Birch plywood
Hinges	1 pr. self-closing, semi-concealed	

Cut face pieces to size and length. Locate all pieces in proper relation to each other and mark the face for dowel locations. See Fig. 6-81. The drawer opening for kitchen cabinets is normally 5½ inches. Use a dowel jig to drill the dowel holes. A homemade jig may be used, as shown in another section. Drill with the front of the facing always in the same direction so the dowels will align when put together. Mark drill with masking tape to drill holes ¾ inch deep. See Fig. 6-82. Carry out sanding of front of facing before gluing. Mark ends of rails to match stiles. See Fig. 6-83 (p. 222).

Fig. 6-79. Pairs of cabinet sides with cleat construction.

Fig. 6-80. Basic box complete for kitchen cabinet.

Fig. 6-81. Facing cut and marked for drilling.

Fig. 6-82. Drilling facing for dowels; masking tape marks depth.

Fig. 6-83. Rails and stiles marked to assure proper location.

This will ensure the same relationship as when drilling. Glue and clamp facing. Be sure the structure pulls together square.

Drill the facing to attach to the cabinet. Nail and glue to partitions. Construct the side guides as shown. See Fig. 6-84. Install in the drawer opening so that the top edge is 2¼ inches below the top of the drawer opening. See Fig. 6-85. The basic cabinet is now

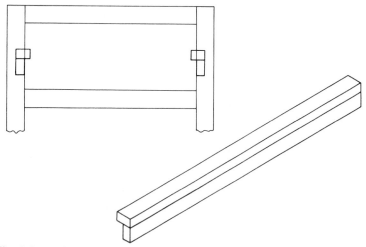

Fig. 6-84. Side guides for kitchen cabinet.

Fig. 6-85.   Side guides protrude ½″ into drawer opening.

complete. See Fig. 6-86. The back will be attached with nails after finishing and installing the top.

Construct the drawer with rabbet joints and side guides. A simple box drawer and side guides are shown further on in this chapter. Construct as shown, with the 5-inch drawer suspended in the center of the 5½-inch opening. Fit the drawer to the space between the side guides, with ⅛-inch play to allow easy movement.

The basic cabinet can be completed with any of a number of door styles. Here a modern overlay door and drawer front have been chosen. See Fig. 6-87. The facing and cabinet exterior have

Fig. 6-86.   Cabinet complete with facing and side guides.

Fig. 6-87.   Finished cabinet with overlay drawer and door.

been stained a medium brown. The door and drawer front are painted a sunshine yellow enamel. No handles are needed, since the edges are beveled back. The drawer has a finger recess underneath. Hinges are self-closing.

Furniture pieces are made with ends of solid wood, of hardwood veneered plywood, or of frame and panel construction. The use of plywood takes advantage of the large, flat surfaces with matched grain. In this type of case work the structural support is provided by skeleton frames.

In constructing a chest, a dresser, or the dry sink shown, the sides are first laid out and cut out of plywood. See Fig. 6-88. Grooves

Fig. 6-88.   Dry sink with large surfaces made of plywood.

are cut in the sides to accept skeleton frames. Cut on a radial arm saw or with a router. Cut a ⅜-by-¼-inch-deep rabbet on the edge of the outside pieces for the back. Skeleton frames should be constructed of ¾-by-1½-inch pine material. Cut a ¼-by-⅜-inch-deep groove along one edge of each part. Cut identical grooves in the ends of the stiles. Use a fixture to hold the pieces upright when cutting on the table saw. If a dust panel is desired, it is placed in the groove already cut. See Fig. 6-89. Glue spline in grooves to assemble frames. Skeleton frames may also be assembled with dowels. The basic case for this type of project is a box with plywood surfaces and skeleton frames. See Fig. 6-90.

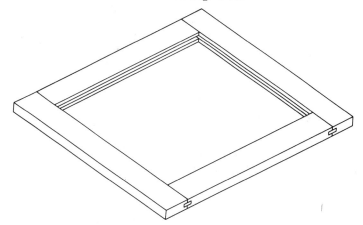

Fig. 6-89.   Skeleton frame construction with splines.

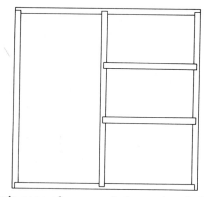

Fig. 6-90.   Basic case of veneered plywood and skeleton frames.

The basic case is completed with the addition of the appropriate trim. The facing is ¾-inch-thick material assembled with dowels. This forms the desired door and drawer openings. Attach to the case with glue and finish nails. Predrill the facing. The base trim is glued over the facing after it is shaped and fitted. The overlap is at least ¾ inch to allow a secure glue joint. Butt joints of the top box are doweled. The basic structure is completed with drawer runners. See Fig. 6-91. Doors and drawers complete the Early American dry sink. See Fig. 6-92.

The cabinetmaker may wish to make the entire cabinet of solid wood. This is necessary when a design is cut on the ends. See Fig. 6-93. In this case, solid wood pieces will be edge glued to form the side surfaces. If possible, purchase surfaced material so that only scraping and sanding are necessary after gluing. A small jointer will be sufficient to develop registration edges.

First prepare end surfaces. Cut dado and rabbet joints in the sides to receive skeleton frames and shelf. Make all joints blind on the front. Cut a ⅜-by-¼-inch-deep rabbet along the back edge for the plywood back. After the joints are cut, lay out the pattern and cut ends to shape.

Fig. 6-91.   Basic case complete with trim.

Fig. 6-92.   Early American dry sink.

Fig. 6-93.   Bedside table made with solid wood.

Skeleton frames are again constructed of ¾-by-1½-inch-material. In the solid wood case the front rail of the frame is made of hardwood to match the cabinet; here maple is used. Cut a notch in the front of the skeleton frame to fit into the blind joints. See Fig.

6-94. The solid wood shelf is also notched. Make a trial run with clamps and no glue to see if all parts fit well. They should all be flush on the front. Glue and clamp to complete the basic case. See Fig. 6-95.

The case is finished with the addition of the appropriate trim. The router is used with a ⅜-inch rounding over bit to shape the top surface. Lower the bit to create the square edge above the round.

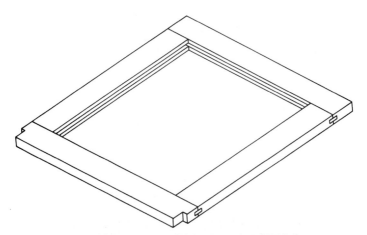

Fig. 6-94. **Skeleton frame notched to make blind joint.**

Fig. 6-95. **Basic case with exposed surfaces of solid wood.**

Cut the apron pieces to fit with miters on the front corners. Use the same bit in the router/shaper table to shape the edge of the apron pieces.

Attach apron pieces to the basic case with glue and screws. The apron should extend out ¾ inch from the sides and front of the case. Slant drill through the top skeleton frame and attach the top with screws.

The sculptured feet are cut from stock made with a cove cut on the table saw. The workpiece is passed sideways over the blade. Start with a shallow cut and make successively deeper cuts. See table saw operations in Chapter 4. The workpiece is completed by routing the upper edge. Considerable hand planing and sanding are required to develop a smooth shape.

Make feet by cutting pieces into pairs with miter joints at the corner. Make a pattern of the foot desired. Place it on the foot pieces, trace, and cut to shape. Assemble each foot by gluing to a large block behind the miter joint. See Fig. 6-96. Cleats attached to the upper edges of the feet hold them to the underside of the apron.

The cabinet is completed with addition of drawers. See Fig. 6-97. A lip type of drawer is used to conform to the Early American style. The drawers are of pine and made as a basic box with the decorative front attached with screws. No additional guides are necessary since each drawer is sliding on the skeleton frame and surrounded by the basic cabinet structure. The cabinet is stained a medium brown and finished with several coats of antique oil finish.

Modular shelving units and cases incorporate hardwood-

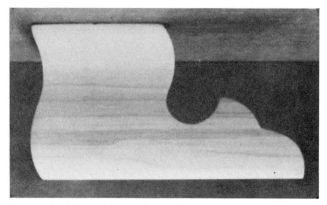

Fig. 6-96.   Sculptured feet made with large corner block.

Fig. 6-97. Bedside table made with solid wood.

veneered plywood. The basic boxes of these structures have the four sides made of plywood. Each box is finished on all sides, so the boxes can be rearranged, allowing for multiple uses. They may be open bookcases or display cases, or made with sliding glass or wooden doors. The units are often used for room or area dividers.

Begin construction by cutting the pieces for the box that will be the base. See Table 6-2 (p. 232). The hardwood-veneered plywood is used for three sides of this box. The large sheet can be broken down, as explained earlier. Be sure the face surface is not chipped during cutting. Joint finished edges that will eventually be faced. See Fig. 6-98.

These boxes may be constructed with rabbet joints or miter joints at the corners. The rabbet joint will show on the sides of the base, but will not be seen on the upper boxes. The miter joints make a good-looking joint, but they must be strengthened with a spline. See Fig. 6-99. This structure has been made with rabbet joints at the corners for ease of construction.

Cut joints on the top and side pieces. Rabbets will be cut on the ends of the top. Cut these ¾ by ⅜ inch deep. Side pieces will have a dado placed even with the notch for the toeboard. Cut these ¾ by ⅜ inch deep. These pieces will have a rabbet along the back

Table 6-2. Wall Furniture Material List

Dimensions are finished sizes.

Case		
Top	1 pc. ¾" × 20" × 36"	Birch plywood
Sides	2 pc. ¾" × 20" × 23⅝"	Birch plywood
Shelf	1 pc. ¾" × 19¾" × 35¼"	Fir plywood
Back	1 pc. ¼" × 23⅝" × 35¼"	Birch plywood
Toeboard	1 pc. ¾" × 3½" × 36"	Birch plywood
Doors	2 pc. ¾" × 16⅞" × 19"	Birch plywood
Center brace	1 pc. ¾" × 2" × 19"	Birch plywood
Front trim	1 pc. ¾" × 12'	Commercial banding
Back trim	1 pc. ¾" × 7'	Commercial banding
Display Unit		
Top and bottom	2 pc. ¾" × 12" × 35¼"	Birch plywood
Sides	2 pc. ¾" × 12" × 18"	Birch plywood
Back	1 pc. ¼" × 17¼" × 35¼"	Birch plywood
Front trim	1 pc. ¾" × 9'	Commercial banding
Back trim	1 pc. ¾" × 9'	Commercial banding
Bookcase		
Top and bottom	2 pc. ¾" × 12" × 35¼"	Birch plywood
Sides	2 pc. ¾" × 12" × 36"	Birch plywood
Shelves	2 pc. ¾" × 11¾" × 35¼"	Birch plywood
Back	1 pc. ¼" × 35¼" × 35¼"	Birch plywood
Front trim	1 pc. ¾" × 18'	Commercial banding
Back trim	1 pc. ¾" × 12'	Commercial banding

edges for the back. Cut this ⅜ by ¼ inch deep. Cut the ¾-inch joints on the radial arm saw with a dado head. This will prevent splitting the veneered surfaces. Cut in from both edges to reach the entire width. Cut all joints with a router if machines are not available. See Fig. 6-100.

Cut the lower shelf and make a trial run with clamps and no glue. Glue and clamp four sides of the basic box. Be sure the case is square when complete. Glue toeboard in place. Attach the back with small brads.

All plywood edges are trimmed with commercial hardwood banding. Cut to length with miter joints at the corners. Glue in place with contact cement. A light sanding of sharp edges is necessary to complete the trim. Trim on the back is carried out in the same manner to hide rabbet joints. Install flush doors of plywood with butt hinges.

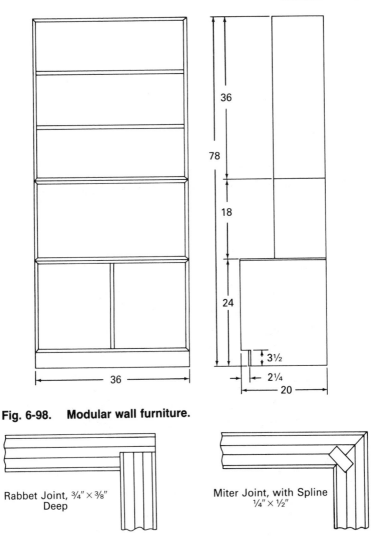

Fig. 6-98. Modular wall furniture.

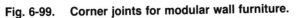

Rabbet Joint, ¾" × ⅜"
Deep

Miter Joint, with Spline
¼" × ½"

Fig. 6-99. Corner joints for modular wall furniture.

Cut material for the top units. Make rabbet joints on the ends of the sides. Place grooves for the shelves of the top unit. All joints are ¾ by ⅜ inch deep. Cut a rabbet on the back edge of the tops, bottoms, and sides for the back. Cut this ⅜ by ¼ inch deep. See Fig. 6-101.

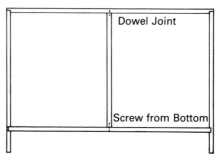

Dowel Joint

Screw from Bottom

Fig. 6-100.   Basic case with joints.

Fig. 6-101.   Joints on upper cases.

Assemble the top units with glue and clamps, making sure they are square when complete. A slight realignment of bar clamps will rack cases into squareness. Attach the back with small brads. Install banding with miter joints. Place on the front and back of the cabinet. Sand the sharp edges to complete the trim. The cabinets may be finished with stain and wipe-on oil finish.

Plastic Laminates

Plastic laminates are used on projects that are intended for heavy use, such as kitchen cabinets, vanities, desks, bars, and family room furniture. The material resists heat, chemicals, and stains and is available in many colors and wood grains. Various surface finishes are available, including glossy and matte.

With some practice and a few basic hand tools, the material is easily installed. The laminate is cut with a mini-hacksaw or saber saw with a metal cutting blade. Final trimming is done with a hand plane and metal file. Special carbide bits are available to use when trimming with a portable router.

The surface to be covered should be particleboard or plywood. Do not use solid wood, which will shrink and swell. Prepare the surface carefully. Make sure it is the exact size desired, and smooth on all surfaces where the laminate will be applied. Note that a single ¾-inch surface is used on some projects. Others require that the plywood be doubled up around the edges. Carefully glue and nail the pieces to get a 1½-inch-thick top. Fill any holes with wood patch, and sand flat and square.

Measure the laminate needed and lay out with pencil on the sheet. Have the good side up if cutting is to be done with a mini-hacksaw; have the good side down if cutting is to be done with the saber saw. See Fig. 6-102. This saw cuts on the upward stroke. Support securely so that laminate does not split or crack. Allow at least a ¼-inch overhang on all edges. Final trimming will be done after bonding.

Apply contact adhesive to the material with a brush. See Fig. 6-103. Apply a liberal coat to both surfaces. Two coats will be needed on the porous wood surfaces. Allow to dry between coats. When surfaces are dry to the touch, contact for permanent bond. Follow the directions for the adhesive used.

When the adhesive is dry and ready to contact, place paper between the large surfaces. See Fig. 6-104. Align the laminate so that each edge overhangs. Slip the paper out in the center area and allow to contact. The material cannot be moved after contact. Remove the remaining paper by lifting the ends of the laminate slightly, and allow to bond. Tap a block of wood with a hammer to secure the bond, starting at the center and working out so that no air is trapped.

If the project is to have edges covered with laminate, this should be done first; this is the case for the backsplash on kitchen cabinets

Fig. 6-102. Cutting the laminate to rough size.

Fig. 6-103. Applying contact adhesive.

Fig. 6-104.   Aligning laminate on base.

Fig. 6-105.   Place laminate on vertical surfaces first.

and vanities. Place the laminate on the vertical surfaces first. See Fig. 6-105. Bond to the ends and trim square and true. Bond to the face and trim square and true. See Fig. 6-106. Use butt joints, with one overlapping the other. Add the horizontal surface last. See Fig.

Fig. 6-106. Place ends and then cover with face piece.

Fig. 6-107. Place horizontal piece last.

6-107. Bond all surfaces securely by tapping a block of wood with a hammer. See Fig. 6-108.

Use a plane to trim off large quantities of excess laminate. See Fig. 6-109. To finish, file all exposed edges at a slight angle with a mill file. Remove all sharp edges. See Fig. 6-110. All other edges are filed square, to be covered.

Remove excess cement at the edges by scraping with a scrap of the laminate. Clean with the solvent used for the contact cement. Use caution—these solvents are highly flammable. Recheck all exposed edges to make sure they are filed smooth.

To master the skills needed to apply the plastic laminate, it is a good idea to practice with scrap pieces. After a little practice constructing some small projects, considerably larger and more complicated projects can be handled with ease.

Doors

The final step in the construction of cabinets is doors and matching drawer fronts. See Figs. 6-111 and 6-112. The doors are attached to the edges of the case or the facing. Doors are most easily made

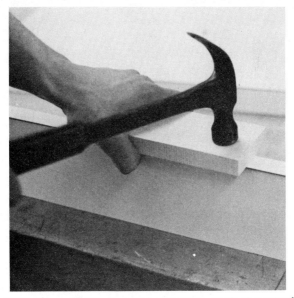

Fig. 6-108.   Tap with block and hammer to contact securely.

Fig. 6-109. Plane off large quantities of waste.

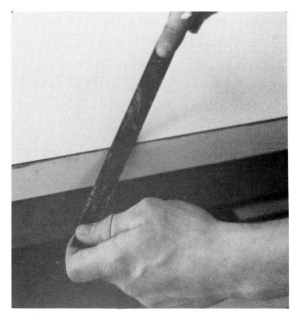

Fig. 6-110. Files edges flush and with a bevel.

Fig. 6-111. Frame and panel doors cover entire cabinet front.

Fig. 6-112. Match door and drawer front on kitchen cabinet.

of plywood. Softwood plywood is often covered with other materials, or painted. See Fig. 6-113. Hardwood plywoods need only trim on the edges. In many cases, additional trim is placed on the front surface. See Fig. 6-114. Doors may be made with rails and panels, but this is much more difficult. See Fig. 6-115.

There are basically three types of doors. See Fig. 6-116. Doors that cover the opening are called overlay doors. Some doors fit only slightly over the opening with a lip, and are called lip-type doors. Flush doors fit in the opening where a flush appearance is desired. The furniture style will dictate the appropriate door front to install.

Modern cabinets usually employ an overlay door. See Fig. 6-

Fig. 6-113.   Painted kitchen cabinets made of plywood.

Fig. 6-114. Raised trim on cabinet doors, made with a router and glued in place.

Fig. 6-115. Frame and panel door of pine, painted for accent.

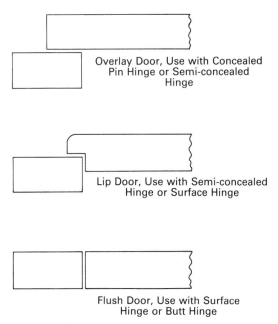

Overlay Door, Use with Concealed
Pin Hinge or Semi-concealed
Hinge

Lip Door, Use with Semi-concealed
Hinge or Surface Hinge

Flush Door, Use with Surface
Hinge or Butt Hinge

Fig. 6-116. Three basic types of doors.

117. This door fits over the door opening. It is made of plywood, with the appropriate edge treatment. Installation is extremely easy.

Ordinarily the door is 2 inches larger in each direction than the opening, with an overlay of 1 inch on all sides. This leaves ½ inch of the 1½-inch facing exposed. The facing width can be adjusted to allow more, less, or no facing showing. On some cabinets the lap is on three sides, with the bottom flush.

The door may be installed with a concealed pin or semi-concealed hinge. See Figs. 6-118 and 6-119. The semi-concealed hinge is easy to install and most convenient if a self-closing type is used. Install the hinge on the door with screws included. Hold the door on the frame with proper spacing, and screw in place. A latch is not needed in this case.

The concealed pin hinge needs a slot cut on the top and bottom of the door. See Fig. 6-120. Place the hinge flush on the door and mark the position. See Fig. 6-121. Cut mortise ³⁄₁₆ inch deep with a hacksaw. Install the hinge on the door. Hold the door on the frame with the proper spacing. Tap lightly to make a mark with the hinge point. Screw in place. Slotted-holes allow for further adjustment.

Fig. 6-117. Overlay door of hardwood plywood with solid wood trim.

Fig. 6-118. Concealed pin hinge on overlay door.

The lip type of door is often used on Early American furniture and cabinets. The door is easily installed and fitted. See Fig. 6-122. It is made to cover the door opening, but has a rabbet around the edge so that it partially protrudes into the opening. The door may be made of plywood or solid wood.

Fig. 6-119.   Semi-concealed hinge on lip door.

Fig. 6-120.   Two types of concealed pin hinges: Flap type requires
1″ overlap; tab type requires ¾″ overlap.

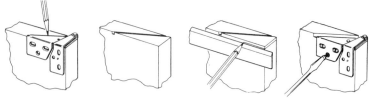

Fig. 6-121.   Steps in installing concealed pin hinge.

Fig. 6-122. Lip-type shutter door with surface hinges.

This door should be made ½ inch larger in each direction than the opening. When installed, this leaves a lip of ¼ inch on all sides overlapping the facing. A ⅜-by-⅜-inch rabbet is cut on the back edges to allow for adjustment. A double door receives rabbets on only three sides. The front edges of this door are rounded or beveled.

Hinges used may be semi-concealed, with a step to fit the rabbet. See Figs. 6-123 and 6-124. Surface hinges that are raised to accommodate the door may also be used. See Figs. 6-125 and 6-126. The hinge is first installed on the door. Place the door in the opening with a ⅛-inch spacer raising the door at the bottom. Screw in place on the facing or door frame.

Fig. 6-123. Semi-concealed hinge placed in a ⅜″ rabbet on lip door; cleat keeps solid pine door flat.

Fig. 6-124. Two types of semi-concealed hinges, for use on lip doors with ⅜″ rabbet and overlay door.

A flush door is used where a clean appearance is desired between the door and the opening. The entire door fits inside the opening. See Fig. 6-127. Often a frame and panel door is mounted flush in the opening. See Fig. 6-128. The flush door takes considerably more time to install.

When installing the door, first check the opening for squareness. Carefully trim the door to fit. A ¹⁄₁₆-inch space should be left on all sides. With the door in the opening, mark the frame and door

Fig. 6-125.   Lip door installed with raised surface hinge.

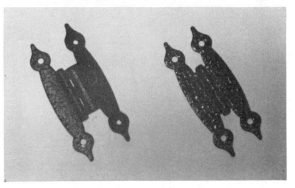

Fig. 6-126.   Two types of surface hinges, for use on lip door and flush door.

Fig. 6-127.   Flush door with plain butt hinges.

Fig. 6-128.   Frame and panel door with decorative butt hinges.

for hinge location. Lay out complete hinge size on the edge of the frame and door. See Fig. 6-129. Cut a gain for the hinge with a chisel. See Figs. 6-130 and 6-131. First cut around the edges to the depth of the hinge leaf. Clean out the gain to receive the hinge. Screw the hinge on the door and then make matching holes on the frame. Place one screw in each side of the hinge so that any further adjustment can be made easily. The gain may need to be slightly deeper to center the door. If the gain is too deep, the hinge can be shimmed with cardboard. Plug screw holes with match sticks if they

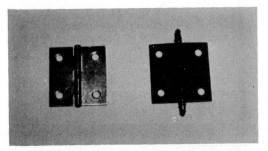

Fig. 6-129. Two types of butt hinges, plain and decorative.

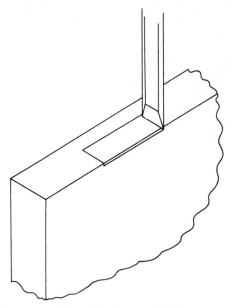

Fig. 6-130. Lay out gain and cut around edges.

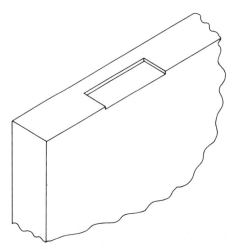

Fig. 6-131.   Complete gain the depth of hinge leaf.

need adjustment. See Figs. 6-132 and 6-133. Flush doors may also be installed with surface hinges.

Various types of catches may be used to hold doors closed. These may employ friction, springs, or magnets. The magnetic type of catch is superior to many others. Semi-concealed hinges with a self-closing device make catches unnecessary.

Fig. 6-132.   But hinge in place, edge of pin on edge of door. Adjust depth to center door in opening.

Fig. 6-133.   Properly placed plain butt hinge.

In some cabinets, sliding doors may work best. These are often used where space is limited and hinged doors will be interfered with. A sliding door is normally made of hardboard. Plastic or metal tracks are used. The tracks are mounted with deeper grooves at the top so that the doors can be removed. Recessed or flat pulls are used.

Drawers

Drawers are an integral part of many cabinetmaking projects, needed in tables as well as in many case goods. See Figs. 6-134 and 6-135. The drawer is made to match the style of furniture and large enough to fill the needs of the project. They may vary from shallow game drawers to extremely deep storage drawers. See Figs. 6-136 and 6-137.

There are basically three types of drawer fronts: overlay, lip, and flush. See Figs. 6-138, 6-139, and 6-140 (pp. 256–57). The front is made to match the doors of the case or the style of the item. For convenience, the drawer fronts should be machined at the same time the doors are made, so that setups will not have to be repeated.

Fig. 6-134. Drawer in end table made to look like three small drawers.

Fig. 6-135. Drawers in wall cabinet.

Fig. 6-136. Shallow game drawer in coffee table.

Fig. 6-137. Deep storage drawer in platform bed.

Fig. 6-138.   Overlay drawer in kitchen cabinet.

Fig. 6-139.   Lip drawer with rounded edge.

Fig. 6-140. Entertainment center with flush drawers.

A drawer should be thought of as basically an open box. The box can be easily made with four sides, a bottom, and a decorative front. See Fig. 6-141. The box structure made with rabbet joints is the simplest drawer to construct. It is made with two identical sides and an identical front and back. See Fig. 6-142. Other construction methods require the front and back to be made quite different from one another. See Fig. 6-143.

A simple drawer structure can be made of pine, usually of ½-inch-thick material. Larger drawers would be ¾ inch thick or made of plywood. The rabbet joints are cut on the sides. Cut them ½ by ¼ inch deep in the ½-inch stock. Cut a ¼-by-¼-inch groove for a

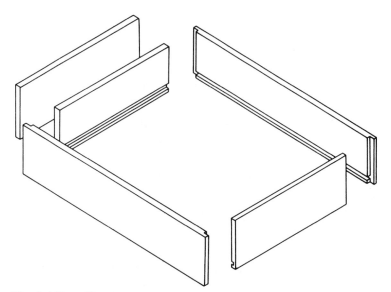

Fig. 6-141.   Simple box drawer structure.

Fig. 6-142.   Lip drawer from simple box with identical parts.

hardboard bottom. Place the groove ¼ inch up from the bottom edge of the sides, front, and back. The drawer should be constructed so that there is a minimum clearance of ¼ inch above the drawer and ¹⁄₁₆ inch on both sides. The drawer should never fit snugly in the drawer opening.

The basic box is assembled with glue and finish nails. See Fig. 6-144. The bottom panel is held securely in the grooves without need for glue. To avoid distortion, the length and width of the panel

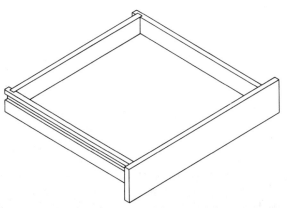

Fig. 6-143.   Overlay drawer with different front and back.

Fig. 6-144.   Simple box drawer, rabbet joints glued and nailed. Note slots for side guides.

should not hit the bottom of the groove. Be sure to check squareness before assembly.

The drawer front can be made to match any style. It is screwed to the front of the box from inside. See Fig. 6-145. It may be located

Fig. 6-145.   Drawer front of any style screwed on from inside.

in any position desired. In some cases this will be flush with the bottom. Other drawers will require a lip type or overlay drawer front of various sizes.

The drawer may be guided by several means. Many of the guide mechanisms can easily be made by the woodworker. Several styles that are attached to the case and drawer are also commercially available. In all cases, the size of the drawer and the weight of the contents must be considered when making a choice. The guide mechanism must make it easy to push the drawer in and out. It must also keep the drawer from tipping down as it is pulled out.

The simplest type of guide system is to fit the drawer to the opening created by the sides and skeleton frames of the case. The weight of the drawer rests on the skeleton frames. The upper skeleton frame acts as a kicker to keep the drawer from tipping. Wax on the bottom of the drawer will help it run easily in the enclosure around it. A center guide may be employed to help the drawers stay aligned. See Fig. 6-146. Here the bottom of the drawer is fitted with a groove for location. See Fig. 6-147. This may be made by gluing two ¼-inch-thick pieces to the bottom of the drawer.

When a wider facing is employed on the cabinet, corner guides must be used. See Figs. 6-148 and 6-149. These hold the weight of

Fig. 6-146. Center guide glued and nailed to skeleton frame.

Fig. 6-147. Strips on bottom of drawer to hold center guide.

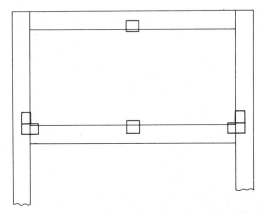

Fig. 6-148. Corner guides, kicker, and center guide attached to skeleton frames.

Fig. 6-149. Corner guides in a small cabinet.

the drawer and direct the movement. A kicker is placed on the structure above to keep the drawer from tipping. The center guide may also be added to make alignment easier.

A most effective guide is a side guide on the drawer. A groove is cut in the side of the drawer. See Figs. 6-150 and 6-151. This should be halfway through the drawer side. A strip of wood is screwed inside the cabinet on which the drawer slides. This centers

Fig. 6-150. Drawer with groove on side fits side guide.

the drawer, carries the weight, and acts as a kicker, all in one. The groove should be made slightly wider than the strip of wood to make movement easy.

Small adjustment of drawers may be made in the opening with the use of thumbtacks. These provide a friction-free surface and lift the drawer slightly where needed. Use wax or spray to free sticky metal parts and eliminate drag between wood surfaces.

If commercial runners are used, these should be purchased before making the drawer. Some require side clearance and necessitate making the drawer 1 inch narrower than the drawer opening. Others require extra clearance in height and depth. These metal or plastic runners are convenient and easy to install.

Fig. 6-151.   Groove in drawer side for guide.

Fasteners

The types of fastener available at the local hardware store are many and varied. Each different job will often require a different fastener; guidance will be provided by the material supplier or the product directions. The fasteners needed in cabinetmaking are limited to very few kinds.

The easiest method of assembly is with nails. They come in a great variety of types, sizes, and gauges. See Tables 6-3 and 6-4. In cabinetmaking the nail is used to hold parts in place while the glue sets. The types most often used are box nails, finish nails, and brads.

The box and the common nail are very similar. The box nail has a large head, but is thinner. This nail holds well, especially when coated. The thin shank permits it to be used without splitting the cabinetmaking material. The finish nail is used where the head needs to be hidden. The head is small, the shank thin. The head is often set below the surface with a nail set. When placing trim with finish nails, it is recommended that a hole be drilled to avoid splitting the thin pieces.

Table 6-3. Size, Gauge, and Number per Pound of Common, Box, and Casing Nails

Penny Size	Length in Inches for Common, Box, and Finish*	Common Nails			Box and Casing Nails		
		Gauge	Thickness in Thousandths	Number per Pound	Gauge	Thickness in Thousandths	Number per Pound
2d	1	15	.072	876	15½	.069	1010
3d	1¼	14	.083	568	14½	.078	635
4d	1½	12½	.102	316	14	.083	473
5d	1¾	12½	.102	271	14	.083	406
6d	2	11½	.115	181	12½	.102	236
7d	2¼	11½	.115	161	12½	.102	210
8d	2½	10¼	.131	106	11½	.115	145
9d	2¾	10¼	.131	96	11½	.115	132
10d	3	9	.148	69	10½	.127	94
12d	3¼	9	.148	63	10½	.127	88
16d	3½	8	.165	49	10	.134	71
20d	4	6	.203	31	9	.148	52
30d	4½	5	.220	24	9	.148	46
40d	5	4	.238	18	8	.165	35
50d	5½	3	.259	14	—	—	—
60d	6	2	.284	11	—	—	—

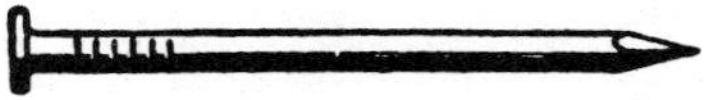

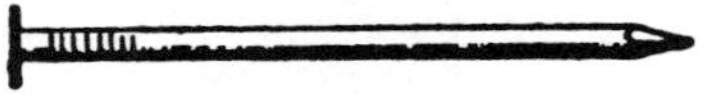

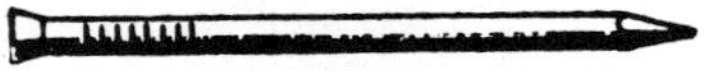

Common

Box

Casing

Table 6-4. Size, Gauge, and Number per Pound of Coated and Finish Nails

Penny Size	Length in Inches for Common, Box, and Finish*	Coated Nails			Finish Nails		
		 Coated			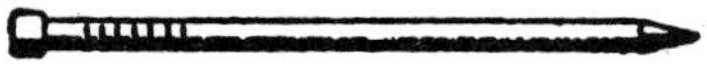 Finish		
		Gauge	Thickness in Thousandths	Number per Pound	Gauge	Thickness in Thousandths	Number per Pound
2d	1	16	.065	1084	16½	.062	1351
3d	1¼	15½	.069	848	15½	.069	807
4d	1½	14	.083	488	15	.072	584
5d	1¾	13½	.088	364	15	.072	500
6d	2	13	.095	275	13	.095	309
7d	2¼	12½	.102	212	13	.095	238
8d	2½	11½	.115	142	12½	.102	189
9d	2¾	11½	.115	130	12½	.102	172
10d	3	11	.120	104	11½	.115	121
12d	3¼	10	.134	77	11½	.115	113
16d	3½	9	.148	61	11	.120	90
20d	4	7	.180	37	10	.134	62
30d	4½	6	.203	29	—	—	—
40d	5	5	.220	21	—	—	—
50d	5½	4	.238	16	—	—	—
60d	6	3	.259	13	—	—	—

*Coated Nails ⅛ inch shorter.

Nails are supplied in lengths with corresponding "penny" size designations. A 1-inch nail is a 2d (two-penny), a 1¼-inch is 3d, a 1½-inch is 4d, and so on. You can usually determine the size needed by measuring the piece being attached. For good holding power, nail through the thinner piece into the thicker one. A rule of thumb is to pick a nail three times as long at the first thickness being fastened, e.g., fasten ½-inch trim with a 1½-inch finish nail.

The brad is a thin nail with a small head. It comes in smaller sizes and thinner gauges than the finish nail. Their small size makes them suitable for delicate work. Small trim, back panels, and other such jobs need brads as fasteners.

A lightweight claw hammer is good for placing small nails. Nail straight, with solid, square blows of the hammer. The nail pattern should be staggered to eliminate splitting. A hole can be drilled by cutting the head off a similar nail and using it as a drill bit. Harder woods will require a fine twist drill bit.

In cabinetmaking projects screws are the main fastener. The screw provides good holding power, and may be used with or without gluing the pieces. If glue is not used, screws permit pieces to be taken apart.

Screws are available in a great number of types, sizes, and gauges. See Figs. 6-152, 6-153, and 6-154. For cabinetmaking a flat-head steel wood screw with a slotted head is most often used. Lengths between ¾ and 1½ inches are commonly used; gauges would be 6, 8, and 10. For special applications the round-head screw may be needed. Placement of hinges is done with both round- and flat-head screws of slotted and Phillips type, made of brass for good appearance.

To get the maximum advantage from screws, they must be properly placed in the wood, which means drilling two holes. The smooth shank requires a hole that the screw can slip into easily. This is drilled in the first piece to be attached, or to the depth the shank will penetrate. A pilot hole is needed for the threaded portion of the screw. This hole is small enough to allow good holding of the threads. When a flat-head wood screw is used, the head must be countersunk. See Fig. 6-155 (p. 271). Use a large bit or special countersink bit. Hold the screw upside down to gauge depth when countersinking. To get a smooth countersink hole, drill it first, then the shank, and finally the pilot hole. To hide the head below the

WOOD SCREW

LENGTHS

Fig. 6-152.   Lengths of flat-head

ACTUAL SIZE CHART

3½   4   4½   5   5½   6

wood screws (actual size).

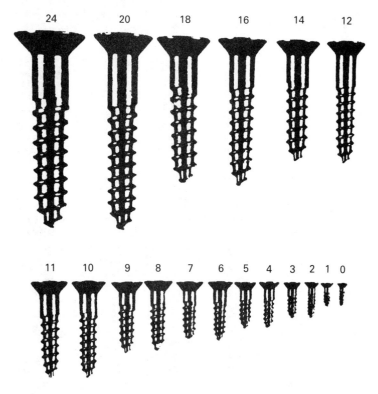

Fig. 6-153.   Gauge sizes of flat-head wood screws.

Slotted   Phillips

Driver Types

Flat   Round   Oval

Head Styles

Fig. 6-154.   Head types and styles of wood screws.

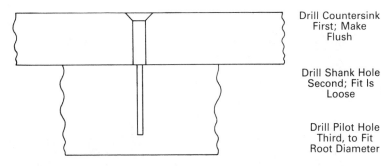

Drill Countersink
First; Make
Flush

Drill Shank Hole
Second; Fit Is
Loose

Drill Pilot Hole
Third, to Fit
Root Diameter

Fig. 6-155.   Countersunk screw holes.

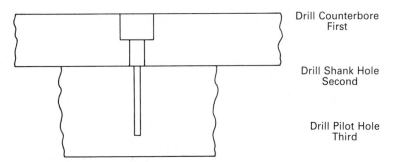

Drill Counterbore
First

Drill Shank Hole
Second

Drill Pilot Hole
Third

Fig. 6-156.   Counterbored screw holes.

surface, counterbore with a large bit and plug or filler over the screw. See Fig. 6-156.

When placing screws, be sure the screwdriver bit fits the head. A small screwdriver will damage the head, one that is too large may damage the wood. A little soap will permit easy placement in the drilled holes. Be sure the holes are large enough for brass screws so they do not twist off. Placing a steel screw first will shape the drilled hole for the brass screw.

Several different kinds of bolt may be needed in cabinetmaking projects: the carriage bolt, the machine bolt, and flat or round-head stove bolts. See Fig. 6-157. The carriage bolt is used where the square part of the head can be imbedded into the wood, which keeps the head from turning and permits it to be close to the surface. These are useful for bolting workbenches and other such structures. The carriage bolt is available in ¼- , ⁵⁄₁₆- , ⅜- , and ½-inch diameters, and lengths up to 12 inches. The machine bolt is used where it is desired to pull up two parts tightly with wrenches. In this case a

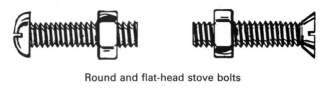

Round and flat-head stove bolts

Hex head machine bolt

Carriage bolt

Fig. 6-157. Various bolts used in cabinetmaking.

socket can be used on the hex head. The machine bolt would be used on large parts that may be taken apart. Sizes are ¼-, ⁵/₁₆-, ⅜-, ⁷/₁₆-, and ½-inch diameters, with lengths up to 12 inches. Stove bolts allow a round or flat head to be used on the surface. These are smaller bolts that would be used to hold together a project such as an easel. A wing nut is often used to facilitate breakdown. Sizes are ⅛-, ³/₁₆-, ¼-, and ⅜-inch diameters, with lengths up to 6 inches.

Large parts that need to be held together securely may be assembled with lag screws. See Fig. 6-158. The lag screw has extremely coarse threads and a hex head. A socket wrench may be used to place this fastener. Sizes are ¼-, ⁵/₁₆-, ⅜-, and ½-inch diameters, with lengths up to 6 inches.

Preparing for Finishing

Preparing the wood surfaces for finishing is a most important step. It can make or break the project and cannot be hurried. Familiarity with the wood is essential. Many defects will become obvious; the wood will have natural defects that need attention, and certain other

Fig. 6-158. Lag screw.

defects may occur during construction and machining that need repair.

The first step is to identify the defects. This is best done by rubbing over the exposed surfaces with a damp cloth. This will darken the wood in the same way as the finish will and defects will become apparent, including dents, scratches, mill marks, and glue marks. The dampening will also raise the grain and permit a better sanding job.

Extremely large defects may require the addition of wood pieces. Where corners have chipped it is possible to plane off the area and apply a new solid wood part. Use a hand plane to get a flat surface. Hold or clamp the new piece until it is dry and work down to the desired shape. A thin piece of wood, such as veneer, can be inserted in a gap to fill an area. Some defects may be drilled out and a solid wood plug used to fill the area. Large dents may be raised with a drop of water, or steamed out with a wet cloth and a soldering copper.

Smaller defects may be removed by scraping, which can easily remove mill marks and scratches and is the best method for removing glue spots. The hand scraper is used on large surfaces. Hold it at a low angle and push forward. A chisel is held in a vertical position for scraping and pulled backward. To remove glue squeeze-out from corners, cut in from two directions flush with the wood. This will cut out most of the glue without damage to the wood. Finish by scraping with the grain.

Other small defects may require commercial or other fillers, which would be used on small cracks and openings or where nails have been set below the surface. Be careful, since these do not take stains well. Some putty and sticks do come in colors to match the finish used. A bit of glue in a defect can be sanded, and the accumulated dust will fill a small defect. Be sure and get all the glue off the surrounding surface. A drop of finish mixed with sanding dust will make a fine putty. This will darken the wood, so use the same one you will use later as a natural finish on the wood.

A smooth, thorough sanding is a final step in preparation. For best results on wood, use garnet or aluminum oxide. This lasts longer and stays sharp. Use a sanding block to keep the surfaces true and square. Sand with the grain. Start with an 80-grit abrasive to shape and remove defects quickly, then use 100, and finally 150 grit to complete this step. Break slightly all sharp edges as a last step in sanding.

When all defects are repaired and sanded, a final raising of the grain is recommended. When the raised wood fibers are dry, a final sanding with 150 grit is necessary. Be careful to do all sanding with the grain. Carry out a final inspection of every inch of the exposed surface.

Finishing

Finishes are used on wood to protect, beautify, and decorate. A great variety of materials is available. Stains are used to provide the desired color, while many transparent finishes protect and paints add accent. The variety of available finishes makes choice somewhat difficult. This depends upon the type and style of cabinetmaking project.

It is important to understand thoroughly material preparation and use. This is done by reading directions carefully and by experimentation. Study the directions and try them out on scrap pieces of the wood. This will develop a feel for the finish and the way it should be applied. Follow all the steps, from proper preparation of the wood to the final application of the finish.

Stains are used to color the wood and accent the grain. Oil stains are the easiest type to use. They go on easily, penetrate slowly, and dry slowly. This makes them easy to control. Stains are available from thin dyes to thick gels.

Mix the stain thoroughly. Apply to a small area, usually a maximum of several square feet at a time, with a brush or rag. Apply evenly and wipe off with a lint-free rag when the color is as desired. Wipe with the grain. Some stains seal on the first coat and color most effectively with a second coat. A very light coat with a controlled amount of stain in a brush will flow out for an even coat. No wiping is then necessary. Oil stains require a 24-hour drying period before other materials are added.

Fillers are used to fill pores of the wood so that a built-up finish can be applied. A paste wood filler is used on open-grained woods. These are available natural or in colors. A liquid sealer is used on close-grained woods.

Mix paste wood filler thoroughly and apply with a stiff brush. The filler should be the consistency of thick cream. Add turpentine to thin if needed. Allow to dry on the wood until it appears dull and work into the pores by rubbing across the grain. Wipe off the excess material by wiping lightly with the grain. Allow 24 hours to dry.

The liquid filler, or sealer, is used to fill the pores of close-grained woods. The sealer also controls finishes, keeping them from combining and stains from bleeding through top coats. Shellac is an excellent sealer under enamel paints. The shellac is thinned with alcohol to give a watery wash coat; several applications are needed. For many synthetic finishes a special sealer is used. Lacquer-base materials require the use of lacquer sealer. Other materials require that the first coat be a thinned-down coat of the finish. Consult the manufacturer's instructions for proper sealing. Be careful to use proper solvents. Lacquer thinner is used with lacquer-base products. Oil-base products require the use of mineral spirits, turpentine, or paint thinner as a solvent.

Finishes are available as top coats or penetrating finishes. The top coats require careful preparation of the wood with fillers and sealers. Carefully sand between coats of sealer and finishes. This smooths any rough areas and helps the next coat adhere. Use a 220-grit abrasive, be careful not to sand through previous coats, which will make undesirable highlights or light areas in the stain. The final coat is often sanded and waxed. Consult manufacturer's instructions for the proper application of the finish.

Penetrating finishes are available in the form of oil finishes, which protect from within the wood and give a more natural look. These are very desirable on the open-grained woods. Apply in a wet coat with a rag and allow to penetrate. Wipe off excess before the finish becomes tacky. Allow to dry 24 hours and sand lightly before applying additional coats. Consult manufacturer's instructions for any variations.

Paints may be used to color cabinets and add accent to a room. Preparation of the wood is equally important when painting. To get a good base, sand well and apply the required sealers, which may be an enamel undercoater. Oil-base paints give a more desirable finish. They are durable under repeated use.

Modern finishes can easily be applied at home with rags or

brushes. Many will be of a wipe-on type. Very good results can be obtained after some experimenting. If you use a brush, be sure to clean it out with several washings of the proper solvent. Wipe it dry and wrap in a paper towel to keep it shaped properly. Keep dust down and materials clean to ensure good results.

CHAPTER 7

The Home Workshop

- ● Space Requirements
- ● Workbenches
- ● Small Workbench
- ● Knockdown Workbench
- ● Hobby Bench
- ● Portable Work Center

- ● Tool Storage
- ● Tin Can Organizer
- ● Tool Tote
- ● Router Table
- ● Electrical Service
- ● Lighting

The value of a home workshop is beyond calculation. The time spent in the shop planning and working gives great peace of mind and contentment. Projects completed will be a source of pride and satisfaction. In many cases these activities, whether building or repairing, will save money. Often the family will become involved in the projects and share in their many advantages.

This section will help to develop an effective workshop. The basic ingredients include a space to work in, a solid work surface, and areas for tool and supply storage. Information is provided so that the workshop can be planned in an orderly fashion. Drawings are included for shop items that can be easily constructed at home, such as benches, storage, and shop aids. Consideration is also given to the electricity and lighting needs of the shop.

Space Requirements

The space devoted to a home workshop can vary greatly, and should depend upon the kinds of projects to be carried out and the amounts of equipment. Woodworking will require considerably more space than tying flies or reloading ammunition. See Fig. 7-1. For this reason, although space requirements can be determined for individual activities or machines, a total square-foot value cannot be given. In any case, the builder will want to estimate his own present and future needs before beginning to develop the shop.

Select a workbench that will fit your needs and locate it against a wall. The benches discussed in this section are all 30 inches deep and of various lengths, from 4 to 7 feet. Tools can be stored on a wall panel above the bench. Avoid placing the bench in a tight corner where work will be cramped. Open space should be provided at each end of the bench for long pieces. See Fig. 7-2. There should be at least 3 feet of work space in front of the bench. A larger open area in front of the bench is convenient for many activities.

Sufficient storage space is a must in any efficient shop. Space must be provided for both large and small items. Determine your storage needs and place shelves from floor to ceiling against a wall. This can easily be made 12 inches deep with shelving boards. See Fig. 7-3. A unit 4 feet wide is appropriate to prevent too much shelf

Fig. 7-1.   Sufficient space in front of bench for woodworking.

Fig. 7-2. Space at end of bench for long pieces.

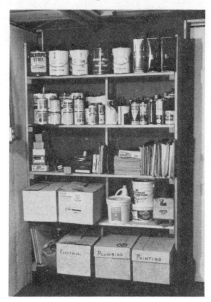

Fig. 7-3. Shop storage.

sag. Space the shelves 12 inches apart and construct them with cleats. Large items and wood can be stored under a bench or vertically in a corner.

Special attention must be paid to the space around the machines. Allow sufficient space to move boards for cutting on the various machines. The table saw needs open space front and back to permit ripping 8-foot pieces. Space on the left side is needed for crosscutting. The radial arm saw may be placed against a wall. Allow space to the right for crosscutting 8-foot pieces. The band saw will need space front and back for cutting long pieces and 6 feet on the right for swinging pieces. Give similar consideration of space requirements to other machines.

Since there is usually not much space available for the home workshop, it is preferable that large pieces be cut out of doors with a portable circular saw. Space problems of machines can best be solved by making them movable. They can then be stored out of the way when not in use. See Fig. 7-4. Retractable casters are avail-

Fig. 7-4.   Jointer stored against the wall.

able commercially for woodworking machines. See Fig. 7-5. These can be purchased for an enclosed steel cabinet or for a steel stand. It is possible to construct wooden benches for machines and place wheels on one end. See Fig. 7-6. The machine is moved, wheelbarrow fashion, to get it out of the way. All machines used in the home shop can easily be set up in this manner.

A second, low bench may be needed in the workshop for a variety of activities. This can be used for such things as clamping and finishing. Bench-type equipment can then be left set up. Sanders and the router table would then be ready for use. See Fig. 7-7.

Fig. 7-5.   Use of retractable casters.

Fig. 7-6.   Movable bench with wheels.

Fig. 7-7.   Low bench for special activities.

Workbenches

Three types of bench are suggested for construction. All vary in basic design, and demonstrate the different possibilities. The small bench is a simple, solid construction. The knockdown bench is an open structure that will appear as a fine piece of woodworking. The bench with cabinet has possibilities as a built-in.

The benches shown also vary in size and height. The 36-inch-high bench is convenient for general activities such as construction, painting, and repair work. The 34-inch height will be serviceable for cabinetmakers who anticipate cutting joints and planing wood clamped to the work surface. The lower bench, made at desk height, will be useful for many hobby activities in which the work is done while sitting down.

Bench lengths vary from 4 feet to 7 feet. These suggested lengths may serve as a minimum and maximum for most home activities. The size of bench depends on the shop space available and the projects to be carried out. In any case, it is better to have excess space than not enough.

Included with any workbench should be devices to hold the work, which are necessary for working with any degree of accuracy. It is also much safer if the work is tightly held and supported. Holding devices may vary from a small clamp or spring-type clothespin, for soldering, to woodworker's or metalworker's vises. See Figs. 7-8 and 7-9. Sawhorses will be needed to cut large plywood panels and boards. Heavy-duty folding sawhorses are available, or they may be made with manufactured brackets of various types. Additional holding devices may be easily constructed in the shop. See Figs. 7-10 and 7-11. The bench hook and miter box will be a great help in cutting small pieces by hand.

Small Workbench

The small workbench provides ample space for small construction activities. Hobby activities and home repair work can easily be carried out in this space. See Fig. 7-12. The overhang on the ends of the bench is wide enough to mount a woodworker's vise underneath. The large drawer and shelf provide considerable storage space. The picture shows a slightly larger bench of this same style. See Table

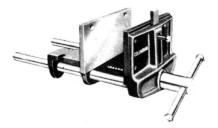

Fig. 7-8. Woodworker's vises.

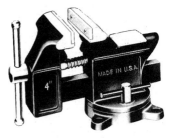

Fig. 7-9. Metalworker's vises.

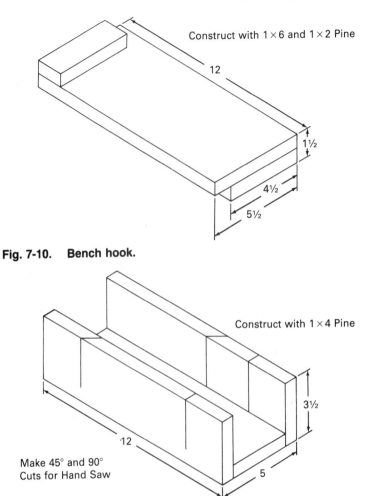

Construct with 1 × 6 and 1 × 2 Pine

12

1½

4½

5½

Fig. 7-10.   Bench hook.

Construct with 1 × 4 Pine

3½

12

Make 45° and 90°
Cuts for Hand Saw

5

Fig. 7-11.   Miter box.

7-1 (p. 287). The work space is 5 feet long, with the space below divided for two storage drawers.

The frame is a bolted construction. See Fig. 7-13. It is made of 2-by-4 stock that has been cleaned up and squared to 1¼-by-3-inch dimensions, which can be done with a jointer and table saw. If this equipment is not available, select straight and clean 2-by-4 material and use as is.

Fig. 7-12.   Small home workbench.

Cut the crossmembers and legs to length. Cut the joints in the legs to the shape shown. A radial arm saw is good for this job. The joints can also be cut with a hand saw or power circular saw. Chisel out the bottom of each joint until it is flat.

Drill the legs and end crossmembers for assembly. Use one 3½-inch bolt at each corner. Place in the middle so it will not interfere with the two bolts that will hold the longer crossmember. Glue these joints and tighten the bolts securely. Make sure the end frames are square. Construct the drawer guide assembly with screws and glue. See Fig. 7-14. Locate each assembly 3 inches down from the top of the end frame. Glue and screw these assemblies to the end frames.

Drill and bolt the long crossmembers in place. Use the 3-inch bolt, and place two at each end, one above and one below the end bolt. Snug up all bolts after the four crossmembers are in place.

The top can be made from two pieces of ¾-inch fir plywood. If reject doors are available from the local lumber yard, cut the top from a solid core door. This makes a very solid work surface. Attach the top to the frame with angle brackets, to avoid any holes in the

Table 7-1. Small Workbench Material List

Dimensions are finished size.

Top		
Surface	2 pc. ¾″ × 30″ × 48″	Fir plywood
Frame		
Legs	4 pc. 1¼″ × 3″ × 34½″	Spruce
Crossmembers	4 pc. 1¼″ × 3″ × 29½″	Spruce
	4 pc. 1¼″ × 3″ × 26″	Spruce
Shelf	1 pc. ¾″ × 26″ × 32″	Fir plywood
Bolts	16 pc. ¼″ × 3″	
	8 pc. ¼″ × 3½″	
Washers	48 pc. ¼″	
Drawer Guide Assembly		
Sides	2 pc. ¾″ × 5½″ × 23½″	Pine
Cleats	4 pc. ¾″ × ¾″ × 5½″	Pine
Side guides	2 pc. ¾″ × ¾″ × 22¾″	Pine
Screws	22 pc. 1¼″ #8 flat head	
Drawer		
Sides	2 pc. ¾″ × 5½″ × 23¼″	Pine
Front	1 pc. ¾″ × 5½″ × 25¾″	Pine
Back	1 pc. ¾″ × 4½″ × 24½″	Pine
Bottom	1 pc. ½″ × 23″ × 24½″	Pine
Handles	2 pc.	

Work Surface 1½″ × 30″ × 48″
  Overhang 8″ on Ends, 2″ Front and Back

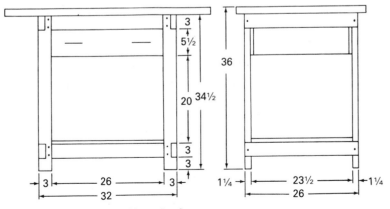

Fig. 7-13. Small workbench plan.

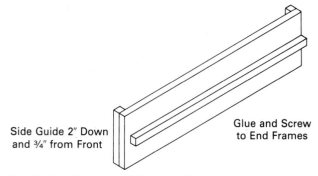

Side Guide 2" Down
and ¾" from Front

Glue and Screw
to End Frames

Fig. 7-14.   Drawer guide assembly.

top surface. Notch the corners of the shelf to fit, and nail in place.

To construct the drawer, nominal size 1-by-6 pine may be used. See Fig. 7-15. Begin with the sides, cutting the groove for the side guide 1¾ inches from the top edge of the pieces. Make sure this will align properly with the side guide. The drawer should have a ¼-inch clearance on the top.

Before cutting the back and front pieces to length, measure

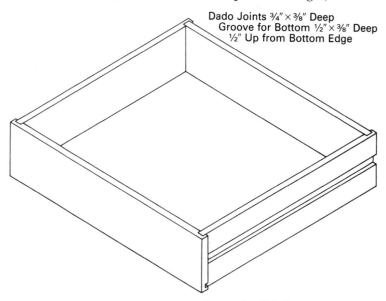

Dado Joints ¾" × ⅜" Deep
Groove for Bottom ½" × ⅜" Deep
½" Up from Bottom Edge

Groove for Side Guide 1" × ⅜" Deep

Fig. 7-15.   Workbench drawer construction.

accurately. Place the sides on the side guides and measure between them. Some variation from the plan may occur, owing to the bolted construction and the type of material used. The finished drawer should have ¼ inch of the side guide fitting into the groove. Drawers will fit flush with the front crossmember.

Cut the drawer bottom. Make a trial assembly of all drawer parts. Nail and glue the drawer together. Attach the front by nailing at an angle through the side pieces. Use a nail set to finish nailing.

Sand all parts of the bench lightly to knock off the sharp corners. Use a clear finish to protect the bench. Attach handles if desired.

Knockdown Workbench

The knockdown workbench is planned to provide a large work area for home projects. See Table 7-2. The bolted construction allows for easy dismantling and moving. The 10-inch overhang on the ends is wide enough to mount a woodworker's vise underneath. See Fig.

Table 7-2. Workbench Material List
Dimensions are finished size.

Top		
Surface	1 pc. 2″ × 30″ × 84″	Maple
Frame		
Legs	4 pc. 2½″ × 3″ × 30¾″	Maple
Top brace	2 pc. 1¼″ × 3″ × 28″	Maple
Rails	2 pc. 1¼″ × 3″ × 58″	Maple
	2 pc. 1¼″ × 3″ × 21″	Maple
Bolts	8 pc. ⅜″ × 5″	
Lag screws	10 pc. ⅜″ × 2½″	
Drawer Guide Assembly		
Sides	3 pc. ¾″ × 5½″ × 26″	Pine
Cleats	8 pc. ¾″ × ¾″ × 26″	Pine
Screws	24 pc. 1¼″ #8 flat head	
Drawers		
Sides	4 pc. ¾″ × 3¾″ × 26″	Pine
Front	2 pc. ¾″ × 5¼″ × 20½″	Maple
Back	2 pc. ¾″ × 3½″ × 19¼″	Pine
Bottom	2 pc. ¼″ × 19¼″ × 25¾″	Fir plywood
Handles	2 pc.	

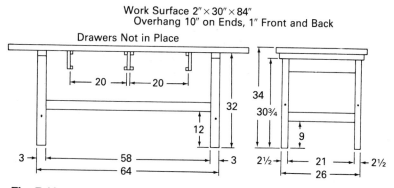

Work Surface 2″ × 30″ × 84″
Overhang 10″ on Ends, 1″ Front and Back
Drawers Not in Place

Fig. 7-16. Knockdown workbench.

7-16. This type of vise can be ordered through many woodworking supply catalogues. Drawer space is provided for valuable woodworking tools.

The material for the frame is hard maple. This should be prepared with the use of a jointer, table saw, and plane. A local lumber mill can prepare the stock. Participation in local Adult Education shop courses will provide the opportunity. The bench can also be made of 2-by-4 spruce, which would be more easily obtained and prepared. Cut all frame members to finished length.

The bench is an open structure that is bolted together. Locate crossmembers at the heights shown. Lay out drill holes to match, and on center. See Fig. 7-17. A ⅞-inch hole is drilled first to receive the nut. The end of the bolt should reach the center of this hole. Drill ⅜-inch holes for all bolts. Drill the top brace for lag screws to attach the frame to the top. Assemble frame with bolts and top brace to frame with lag screws.

The 2-by-30-by-84-inch top is a laminated surface made of maple or spruce. Joint one surface and plane the pieces to uniform thickness. Glue face-to-face into three 10-inch-wide pieces. Approximately seven 2-by-4's will be needed for each section. This will permit ease of handling and will fit machines. Joint and plane to the final thickness for the top surface. Carefully glue and align the pieces to make the completed top.

Attach the top to the frame with lag screws from underneath. Attach a woodworker's vise on the end desired. Drill holes in line with the vise for use of a bench stop. A piece of dowel can be used as the stop.

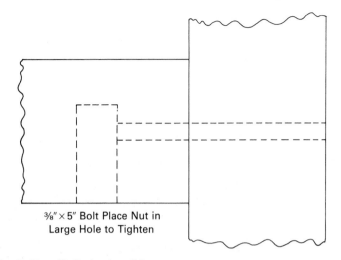

³⁄₈″ × 5″ Bolt Place Nut in
Large Hole to Tighten

Fig. 7-17.   Bolted assembly.

Cut members for the drawers. Make dado joints ¾ by ⅜ inch deep and ¼ inch from the end of the pieces. See Fig. 7-18. The groove for the bottom is ¼ by ⅜ inch deep and ¼ inch from the bottom edge of the sides. Position the groove on the front piece so that the front extends ¾ inch above and below the side. This will cover the guide assembly.

Cut the drawer bottom. Make a trial assembly of all drawer parts. Nail and glue the drawer together.

Sand all parts of the bench lightly to knock off the sharp corners. Use a clear finish to protect the bench. Attach handles if desired.

Hobby Bench

This 30-inch-high bench is designed for carrying out activities while seated. See Fig. 7-19. The bench space is suitable for such construction activities as working on collections and sewing. The drawer space is sufficient to store various supplies. Drawers use metal side guides to support the weight and so that they will roll easily.

The construction of the open frame section is similar to that for the knockdown bench. Leg and crossmembers are held together with bolts. Cut members and legs to size. See Table 7-3 (p. 293). Locate end crossmembers 4 inches from top and bottom, and back crossmember 7 inches high. Lay out drill holes to match, and cen-

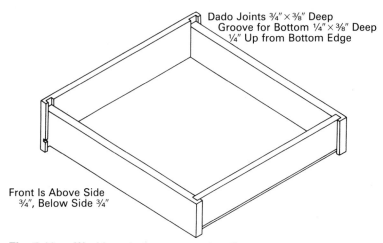

Dado Joints ¾″ × ⅜″ Deep
Groove for Bottom ¼″ × ⅜″ Deep
¼″ Up from Bottom Edge

Front Is Above Side
¾″, Below Side ¾″

Fig. 7-18.   Workbench drawer construction.

Work Surface 1½″ × 30″ × 60″
Overhang 3″ on All Sides

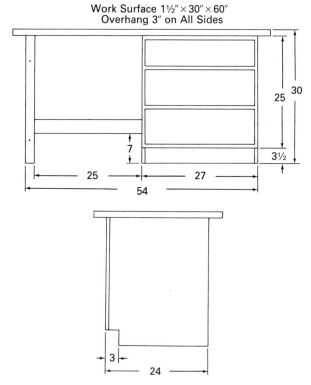

Fig. 7-19.   Hobby bench.

Table 7-3. Hobby Bench Material List
Dimensions are finished size.

Top		
Surface	2 pc. ¾″ × 30″ × 60″	Fir plywood
Frame		
Legs	2 pc. 2″ × 2″ × 28½″	Birch
Crossmembers	2 pc. 1¼″ × 3″ × 20″	Birch
	1 pc. 1¼″ × 3″ × 25″	Birch
Bolts	6 pc. ⅜″ × 3″	
Washers	6 pc. ⅜″	
Case		
Sides	2 pc. ¾″ × 23¼″ × 28½″	Birch plywood
Crossmembers	8 pc. ¾″ × 2″ × 26¼″	Pine
Toeboard	1 pc. ¾″ × 3½″ × 25½″	Birch
Facing	2 pc. ¾″ × ¾″ × 25″	Birch
	4 pc. ¾″ × ¾″ × 25½″	Birch
Screws	16 pc. 1¼″ #8 flat head	
Drawers		
Sides	2 pc. ¾″ × 5¾″ × 24″	Pine
	4 pc. ¾″ × 7¾″ × 24″	Pine
Front, back	2 pc. ¾″ × 5¾″ × 23¾″	Pine
	4 pc. ¾″ × 7¾″ × 23¾″	Pine
Bottom	3 pc. ¼″ × 23¼″ × 23¾″	Fir plywood
Front trim	1 pc. ½″ × 6½″ × 26″	Birch
	2 pc. ½″ × 8½″ × 26″	Birch
Guides	3 pr. 24″ metal side guides	
Handles	3 pr.	

tered. The end of each bolt should reach the center of the larger hole. Drill the ⅞-inch hole first and then the ⅜-inch holes.

Cut case sides, crossmembers, and toeboard. Locate and cut notch in the sides. See Fig. 7-20. Lay out joints for crossmembers. Make sure sides are in pairs and not exact duplicates. Cut joints 3 inches in from the front and back edges. Locate crossmembers in the joints and drill at a slight angle for screws. See Fig. 7-21. Assemble with glue and screws. Install toeboard with finish nails. Be sure the case is square as it is assembled. It can be pulled square before the glue is dry if a problem is noted quickly enough. Machine facing and attach with glue and finish nails. Install metal side guides.

Cut material for the drawers. Make a ¼-by-¼-inch groove for bottom, on all pieces. Place ¼ inch up from the bottom edge. Cut a rabbet ¾ by ⅜ inch deep on the ends of the sides. See Fig.

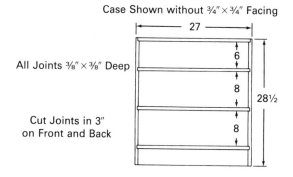

Fig. 7-20. Hobby bench base cabinet.

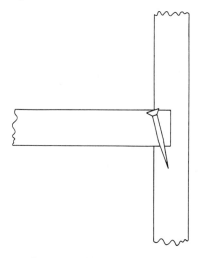

Fig. 7-21. Screw placement in crossmember.

7-22. Cut and fit the bottom. Glue and assemble the drawer with finish nails.

Cut the material for the decorative fronts. Locate the fronts with ¾-inch overhang on both ends and ¼ inch on the bottom. Drill and attach with screws. Install metal side guides.

Cut top pieces and nail together. Assemble the frame with bolts and attach to the case. Attach the top with angle brackets. It may be covered with Formica or hardboard to make a more serviceable work surface.

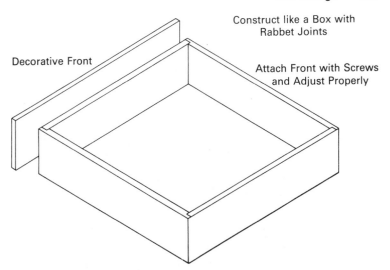

Construct like a Box with
Rabbet Joints

Decorative Front

Attach Front with Screws
and Adjust Properly

Fig. 7-22.   Drawer construction.

Portable Work Center

A commercial work center is available that serves as a giant vise, sawhorse, and work surface, all in one. See Fig. 7-23. The work surface is a convenient 31¼ inches high. Vise jaws open to 5¼ inches and hold tapered objects easily. The long jaws provide an extremely versatile holding device for all types of work.

The work center is portable and is easily folded for carrying. It can be set up in the garage, the workshop, or on the work site. Storage is no problem since the work center folds up flat.

A bench-top work center and clamping device is also available. See Fig. 7-24. It is easily mounted with included clamps or suction cups on any smooth surface. It is extremely useful when working in limited space where a holding device is essential. The vise opens to 5¼ inches and swivels to hold odd shapes. The work surface tilts to hold craft and hobby work.

Tool Storage

Proper storage of tools is an important consideration in the shop. Tools must be easy to grasp, and should also be arranged so as to

Fig. 7-23.   Portable work center. *(Courtesy Black & Decker)*

Fig. 7-24.   Bench-top work center. *(Courtesy Black & Decker)*

be protected while being stored and so cutting edges are not damaged. Proper storage will also permit retrieval without injury. Piling tools in a box or drawer is not a satisfactory solution.

The most effective tool storage method for home use is a pegboard panel. A 4 × 4-foot board ⅛ inch thick is a good size. See Fig. 7-25. Specially designed metal brackets may be purchased for hang-

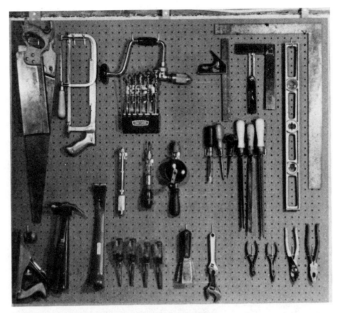

Fig. 7-25.   Tool panel of ⅛″ pegboard.

ing most tools. These brackets permit rearrangement when additional tools are purchased.

A plywood panel can also be used, with nails or dowels used to hang the tools. The plywood panel should be at least ½ inch thick. Special brackets are made from solid wood for screwdrivers, chisels, and files. See Fig. 7-26.

Some craftsmen prefer to store valuable tools in shallow drawers. These may be built into a toolbox or below the workbench. Special brackets and compartments are provided for each tool. This protects the tools from damage, dust, and corrosion.

Tin Can Organizer

The organizer for hardware and small tools is designed according to the size of cans used. See Fig. 7-27. Cans should be large enough to allow easy reaching down inside. This organizer uses 4-inch-diameter by 4¾-inch cans. See Table 7-4 (p. 299).

Enlarge the handle pattern with hand hole well above the tin cans. See Fig. 7-28. Trace pattern on ½-inch-thick wood. Begin by

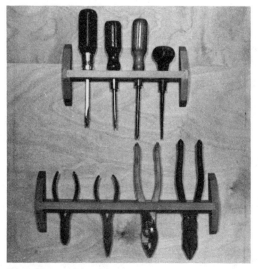

Fig. 7-26.   Wooden tool brackets.

Fig. 7-27.   Organizer for hardware and small tools.

drilling 1-inch holes at each end of the handle hole. Cut between holes with a saber saw. Sand and smooth to finish.

Align tin cans and handle to determine drill location. Drill cans and wood to accept ³⁄₁₆-by-³⁄₄-inch bolts. Attach cans to wood handle. Drill and secure cans to each other with smaller bolts.

Finish is applied to parts when disassembled. The handle has been oiled, cans painted with spray paint.

Table 7-4. Tin Can Organizer Material List
Dimensions are finished size.

Handle	1 pc. ½" × 7" × 8½"	Hardwood
Tin cans	4 pc. 4" dia. × 4¾"	
Bolts	2 pc. ³⁄₁₆" dia. × ¾" round head	
	2 pc. ¼" dia. × ¼" round head	
Abrasive paper		
Oil finish		
Spray paint		

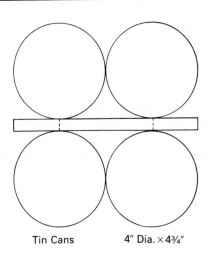

Tin Cans   4" Dia. × 4¾"

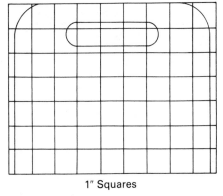

1" Squares

Fig. 7-28. Tin can organizer.

Tool Tote

The tool tote is extremely useful for carrying and storing tools. See Fig. 7-29. It is constructed of standard stock available at any lumber yard. Assembly is carried out with butt joints. All joints should be glued and screwed.

When purchasing material, look for a good grade of pine. See Table 7-5. Be sure the material is flat. Pegboard should be available in partial sheets, 2 by 4 feet.

Cut the pine pieces to 23-inch lengths. Three pieces of the 1-by-6 and the 1-by-12 are needed. Lay out the end pieces as shown. See Fig. 7-30. Cut with a power circular saw and plane smooth.

On the end pieces, find the center location for the pegboard. Cut the molding and glue and nail in place. Allow enough space to slide the pegboard in the slot easily. Locate holes for screws on all pine pieces. Place evenly ⅜ inch in from ends. Drill and countersink for the no. 8 screws.

Begin assembly by attaching the bottom to the ends. Cut pegboard and slide into place. Attach the top piece and attach the sides.

Sand lightly to knock off the sharp corners. Protect the tool tote with several coats of polyurethane finish. Attach handle and organize tool hangers.

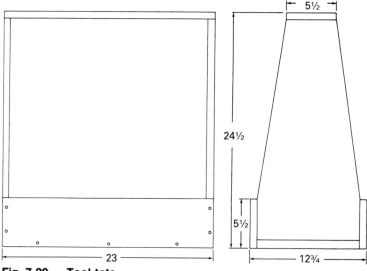

Fig. 7-29.   Tool tote.

Table 7-5. Tool Tote Material List
Dimensions are finished size.

Ends	2 pc. ¾″ × 11¼″ × 23″	Pine
Sides	2 pc. ¾″ × 5½″ × 23″	Pine
Bottom	1 pc. ¾″ × 11¼″ × 23″	Pine
Top	1 pc. ¾″ × 5½″ × 23″	Pine
Tool board	1 pc. ¼″ × 21½″ × 23″	Pegboard
Molding	4 pc. ¼″ × ¾″ × 23″	Pine
Screws	24 pc. 1½″ #8 flat head	
Handle	1 pc. galvanized door handle	
Hangers	Various pegboard hangers	
Abrasive paper		
White glue		
Polyurethane finish		

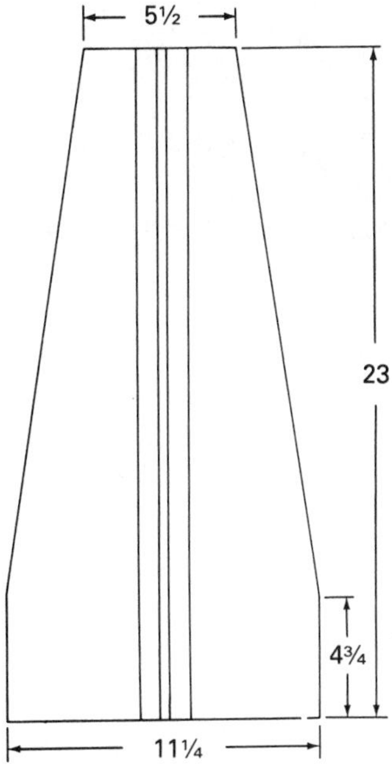

Fig. 7-30. Tool tote—end pattern.

Router Table

The router table will become a very valuable shop tool. With the router held in this position, it becomes much more versatile. See Fig. 7-31. This is very similar to a shaper, and allows safe cutting of small parts. Decorative cuts or joints may easily be cut, with or without the fence. Use the router/shaper with the table clamped to a bench.

Construction is begun by cutting the two top pieces. See Table 7-6. The 6½-inch circle must be cut through the plywood before the boards are glued together. When in use the router is attached

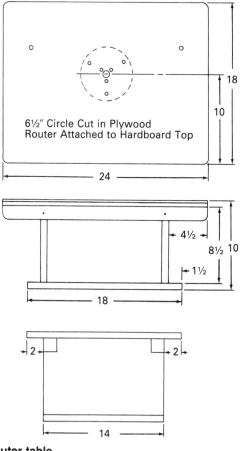

6½" Circle Cut in Plywood
Router Attached to Hardboard Top

Fig. 7-31.   Router table.

Table 7-6. Router Table
Dimensions are finished size.

Table		
Top surface	1 pc. $\frac{1}{4}'' \times 18'' \times 24''$	Hardboard
Second surface	1 pc. $\frac{1}{2}'' \times 18'' \times 24''$	Fir plywood
Braces	2 pc. $1\frac{1}{4}'' \times 1\frac{1}{2}'' \times 24''$	Spruce
Ends	2 pc. $\frac{3}{4}'' \times 8\frac{1}{2}'' \times 14''$	Fir plywood
Bottom	1 pc. $\frac{3}{4}'' \times 14'' \times 18''$	Fir plywood
Screws	20 pc. $1\frac{1}{2}''$ #8 flat head	
Fence		
Base	1 pc. $\frac{3}{4}'' \times 4'' \times 24''$	Pine
Upright	1 pc. $\frac{3}{4}'' \times 3'' \times 24''$	Pine
Machine bolts	2 pc. $\frac{1}{4}'' \times 2''$	
Washers	4 pc. $\frac{1}{4}''$	
Wing nuts	2 pc. $\frac{1}{4}''$	
Screws	4 pc. $1\frac{1}{4}''$ #8 flat head	

directly to the hardboard and the plastic base is removed. Screws that hold the plastic base will hold the router in position. Check your router for the size of the base circle and determine if other areas of the plywood should be cut away for the handle. Glue and clamp the top surfaces together.

Cut out all the remaining parts for the table. The ends are notched to receive the braces. These braces are specifically designed to hold the table flat. Place a 1-inch radius on all outside corners. See Fig. 7-32.

Assembly of the router table is very simple. All joints are butt joints, glued and screwed. Drill for screws and attach the ends to the base. Attach the braces in the notches and attach the top. Sand all sharp corners lightly and apply a clear finish.

Cut the parts for the fence from a good grade of common pine. Cut matching holes in the pieces so the fence will not interfere with bit placement. See Fig. 7-33. Slotted holes are used to allow for easy adjustment of the fence. Drill and cut with a saber saw. Drill for screws and attach upright to base. Drill holes in the tabletop to match location of slots in the fence.

Electrical Service

The modern home uses a great many electrical appliances. When shop equipment is added, the home may have outgrown its wiring.

Fig. 7-32.   Design for router table.

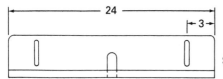

Slotted Holes for Adjustments

Opening in Center of Fence for Blades

Fig. 7-33.   Router table fence.

A 150- or 200-ampere service entrance is needed, for which the appropriate size of entrance switch and entrance wires are necessary. If fuses are blown occasionally or lights dim, have the service checked.

The home workshop should be provided with a separate circuit to supply the many appliances. This should be a 20-ampere circuit. The circuit should be wired with no. 12 wire to carry the maximum 2400 watts. No combination of machines exceeding this wattage should be used at any one time.

Place receptacles at a convenient height for shop use; 42 inches above the floor brings them above the counter. For installations where the walls are block or concrete, it will be necessary to drop a 1-by-4 board from the sill to attach the box and strap the wire. Be sure that grounded receptacles are used and that the box and receptacle are properly wired to ground. A box placed every 6 feet is desirable for shop machines and portable power tools.

Lighting

Light is an important consideration in the home shop. If the shop is not well lighted from natural sources, artificial light must be provided. A well-lighted work area will lessen the likelihood of mistakes and accidents. Smaller and more detailed work will need even more concentrated light.

The recommended light at the work surface of benches and machines is from 25 to 50 foot-candles. This light should be well diffused and without glare, and placed to avoid shadows.

The light provided by fluorescent fixtures is preferable. A 4-foot fixture with two tubes should be placed above each major work area. For more concentrated light at work stations, incandescent bulbs with metal deflectors may be used. These can be adjusted to provide needed extra illumination.

The fixtures should be hung close to the ceiling. It is assumed that most home shops will have an 8-foot ceiling in the basement or garage. Hanging the fixtures as high as possible will help to diffuse the light and eliminate shadows. Hang fixtures by appropriate hangers or chains, not by looping the cord.

Of great help in creating a well-lighted shop is the overall color. If the walls and floor are to be painted, use a light color to reflect light and reduce glare. This will also create a more pleasant work atmosphere.

CHAPTER 8

Projects

- Open Stereo Cabinet
- Speaker Cabinets
- Bookcase
- Office Desk
- Platform Bed

- Kitchen Cabinets, Base
- Upper Kitchen Cabinets
- Bathroom Vanity
- Cubes

Open Stereo Cabinet

The open stereo cabinet has been designed as an example of a structure suitable for a modern music center. The overall size of 20 by 16½ by 46½ inches high is an appropriate size for most equipment. See Fig. 8-1. This size cabinet works well in many settings. In the plan, it is assumed that the spacing of shelves would be adjusted to fit existing equipment and provide record and tape storage. Here record storage is in the bottom. Dividers may be desired in this area. The second space from the bottom is intended for tape storage. A drawer or sliding shelf could be incorporated here. The top three areas are intended for system components.

The cabinet should be made of birch plywood with matching solid wood trim. See Table 8-1. Begin by ripping the plywood sheet into 15½-inch strips to make all parts. One sheet of plywood is needed. Add an allowance to smooth edges on the jointer. Crosscut to the exact length for sides, shelves, and other parts.

Cut joints after all parts have been cut to the exact length, and square. See Fig. 8-2. Cut dado joints ¾ by ⅜ inch deep. This can

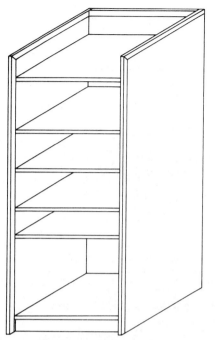

Fig. 8-1.   Stereo cabinet.

be done on the radial arm saw by cutting in from both edges, or with a router.

Make a trial assembly of all parts of the cabinet without glue. Make sure all parts fit well and the cabinet is square.

Table 8-1.   Open Stereo Cabinet Material List
Dimensions are finished size.

Case		
Sides	2 pc. $\frac{3}{4}'' \times 15\frac{1}{2}'' \times 45\frac{1}{2}''$	Birch plywood
Shelves	6 pc. $\frac{3}{4}'' \times 15\frac{1}{2}'' \times 19\frac{1}{4}''$	Birch plywood
Toepiece	1 pc. $\frac{3}{4}'' \times 2'' \times 18\frac{1}{2}''$	Birch plywood
Back	1 pc. $\frac{3}{4}'' \times 2'' \times 18\frac{1}{2}''$	Birch plywood
Facing		
Sides	2 pc. $\frac{3}{4}'' \times 1'' \times 46\frac{1}{2}''$	Maple
Shelves	6 pc. $\frac{1}{4}'' \times \frac{3}{4}'' \times 18\frac{1}{2}''$	Maple
Top	1 pc. $\frac{3}{4}'' \times 1'' \times 18\frac{1}{2}''$	Maple
Top	2 pc. $\frac{3}{4}'' \times 1'' \times 16\frac{1}{2}''$	Maple

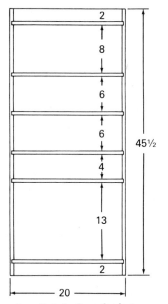

Fig. 8-2. Basic construction before facing.

Assemble the basic cabinet with glue and bar clamps. If only a few clamps are used, finish nails may be used to pull shelves and sides together. Check several times with a square to ensure squareness. Fit the top board and the toeboard snugly, and glue.

A wide facing is added to the front and top. This will give a modern finished look and also allow for the addition of Plexiglas doors. These would fit between the sides of the cabinet. Attach facing with glue and nails. Use miter joints at the top, and butt all other pieces.

Sand all surfaces carefully. Use abrasive paper with a sanding block to keep all corners square. Sand all edges flush and round slightly all sharp corners. Finish with a stain of the desired color and Danish oil finish.

Speaker Cabinets

Many methods may be used to construct a speaker cabinet. Solid wood or hardwood plywood are used to make a top-quality cabinet. This would be constructed with miter joints. See Fig. 8-3. Rabbet

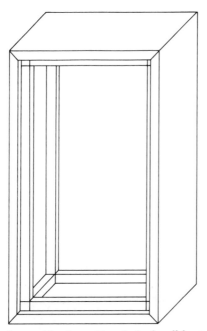

Fig. 8-3. **Speaker cabinet constructed of solid wood or hard plywood.**

joints may be used where appearance is less important. Using cleats is a good way of strengthening joints in either cabinet. Glue and screw the cleats in place. The cabinet must be a solid structure that will not reverberate. A good size is 13 by 23 by 9 inches deep.

An easily made and serviceable cabinet can be constructed of fir plywood and covered with wood-grained contact paper. The cabinet may also be covered with vinyl or wood veneer. Solid wood trim would be desirable on the wood-veneered cabinet.

Cut plywood parts and assemble butt joints with nails and glue. See Fig. 8-4. Glue ¾-inch-square cleats in the corners for additional strength. Corner cleats should be ½ inch short of the back to allow for the ½-inch-thick plywood back. The cleats should be ¾ inch short of the front to allow for ½-inch-thick plywood. The additional distance back will give a frame effect around the front. The front plywood will hold the speaker and should be covered with grill cloth.

Glue cleats on the inside surfaces from corner to corner. Predrill the front cleats for attaching the front panel. Cut the front ⅛ inch

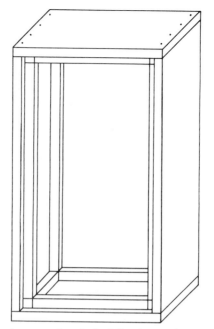

Fig. 8-4. Speaker constructed of fir plywood covered with wood-grained contact paper.

smaller than the opening size so it will fit after covering with grill cloth. Cut hole for speaker and mount. Cover the front panel with grill cloth.

After all the cleats are in, cover the box with wood-grained contact paper. Cut to approximate size. Start at a corner and wrap the paper around the cabinet. Do a little at a time, being careful as you take off the backing and stick the paper down. Rub out all air pockets; keep the paper square. End at a corner, and cut square. Wrap the paper around front and back edges to the cleats.

Finish by screwing front in place from the inside. Complete the necessary wiring. Attach the back with screws.

Bookcase

The Early American bookcase is a free-standing bookcase. It provides space for books, display of valuables, and storage in the base.

See Fig. 8-5. The case is made of fir plywood and pine for inexpensive and easy construction. The project is painted an Early American color that complements the living room decor.

Begin construction by ripping the sides to width. See Table 8-2 (p. 312). Cut the shelves to width. Note the two different widths. Add an allowance to smooth edges on the jointer. Crosscut all pieces to length.

Cut joints after all the pieces have been cut to length, and square. See Fig. 8-6. Cut rabbet and dado joints on the sides ¾ by ⅜ inch deep. This can be done on the radial arm saw, by cutting from both sides, or with a router. Place a ⅜-by-¼-inch-deep rabbet

Fig. 8-5. Early American bookcase.

Table 8-2. Bookcase Material List
Dimensions are finished size.

Case			
Sides	2 pc.	$3/4'' \times 14'' \times 78''$	Fir plywood
Shelves	3 pc.	$3/4'' \times 13'' \times 33\frac{1}{4}''$	Fir plywood
	3 pc.	$3/4'' \times 13\frac{3}{4}'' \times 33\frac{1}{4}''$	Fir plywood
Back	1 pc.	$1/4'' \times 33\frac{1}{4}'' \times 74\frac{3}{4}''$	Fir plywood
Facing			
Vertical	2 pc.	$3/4'' \times 2\frac{1}{2}'' \times 64\frac{1}{4}''$	Pine
Horizontal	1 pc.	$3/4'' \times 13\frac{3}{4}'' \times 34''$	Pine
	2 pc.	$3/4'' \times 2\frac{1}{2}'' \times 29''$	Pine
	3 pc.	$3/4'' \times 3/4'' \times 33\frac{1}{4}''$	Pine
Trim			
Modern base	1 pc.	$1'' \times 4'' \times 34''$	Pine
Quarter round	3 pc.	$3/4'' \times 3/4'' \times 34''$	Pine
Square	2 pc.	$1'' \times 1'' \times 34''$	Pine
Batten	1 pc.	$1/4'' \times 2\frac{1}{2}'' \times 34''$	Pine
	1 pc.	$1/4'' \times 1\frac{3}{4}'' \times 34''$	Pine
Doors			
Vertical	4 pc.	$3/4'' \times 1\frac{3}{4}'' \times 19\frac{1}{2}''$	Pine
Horizontal	6 pc.	$3/4'' \times 1\frac{3}{4}'' \times 11''$	Pine
Panels	2 pc.	$3/4'' \times 5\frac{1}{2}'' \times 11\frac{1}{2}''$	Pine
	2 pc.	$3/4'' \times 9\frac{3}{4}'' \times 11\frac{1}{2}''$	Pine
Splines	8 pc.	$1/4'' \times 1/2'' \times 1\frac{1}{2}''$	Fir plywood
	4 pc.	$1/4'' \times 1/2'' \times 1''$	Fir plywood

on the back edge of the sides. Glue and nail pine facing to the three intermediate shelves. Carry out a trial run for assembly without glue. Assemble the basic cabinet with glue and finish nails. Be sure the cabinet is square when this step is done.

The front facing is made of pine. Cut pieces and attach to cabinet with glue and finish nails. See Fig. 8-7. The top board with arch may have to be glued from several narrow boards to avoid warping. Cut the arch and sand well before attaching.

Trim is placed on over the pine facing. See Fig. 8-8. Each piece is glued and clamped. The case is now complete. All the plywood edges should be covered. The 19½-by-29-inch door opening is ready for doors.

Cut all pine pieces for the doors. Cut a ¼-by-¼-inch deep groove along one edge of each narrow piece. The center stile has a groove on two sides. Cut identical grooves on the ends of the stiles.

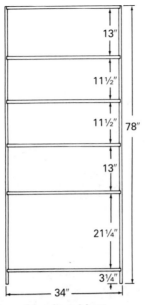

Fig. 8-6.   Construction of basic cabinet.

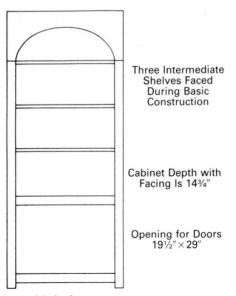

Three Intermediate
Shelves Faced
During Basic
Construction

Cabinet Depth with
Facing Is 14¾″

Opening for Doors
19½″ × 29″

Fig. 8-7.   Basic cabinet with facing.

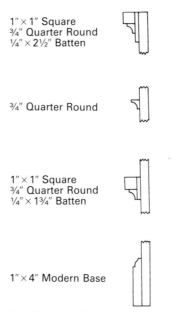

1" × 1" Square
¾" Quarter Round
¼" × 2½" Batten

¾" Quarter Round

1" × 1" Square
¾" Quarter Round
¼" × 1¾" Batten

1" × 4" Modern Base

Fig. 8-8. Trim combinations on front of cabinet.

Use a fixture to hold the pieces upright when cutting on the table saw.

Door panels are cut to shape on the table saw. Set the table saw blade to the appropriate angle and height. Cut panels by holding them on edge and passing along the fence. See Fig. 8-9. The narrow panel may need a backup board to carry it past the blade easily. The second cut is made with the blade square. Set the distance to the fence with the blade at a shallow depth. Lay the panel down to square off the edge of the bevel. Cut the rabbet on the back of the panel. Carefully sand with abrasive paper and sanding block to eliminate saw marks and keep the bevel flat and true. Make sure the edges are not made too narrow to fit the grooves in the frames. See Fig. 8-10.

Carry out a trial assembly without glue on the doors. The panels should fit just loosely enough to allow for future expansion. Place glue on the splines and in the groove, and clamp. The panel should float, with no glue. Carefully check squareness as the doors are set aside to dry.

Finish by fitting doors and attaching hinges, using a butt hinge.

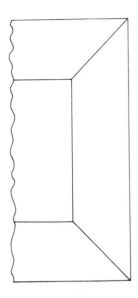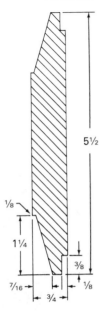

Fig. 8-9.   Detail of door panel.

Fig. 8-10.   Cross section of door.

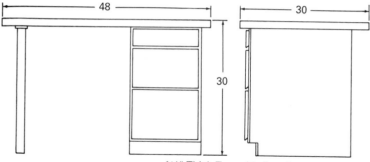

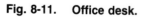

1½"-Thick Top with Formica

Fig. 8-11.   Office desk.

Fig. 8-12.   Base cabinet of office desk.

Set nails and fill holes. Sand all surfaces thoroughly. Slightly round all sharp edges. Undercoat the cabinet several times to prepare a good surface for the final painting. Paint the desired color. Install the back with brads, and attach door hardware.

Office Desk

The office desk is a very simple construction. It has been designed to be functional and not as a decorative piece of furniture. The Formica top provides an ample work surface. See Fig. 8-11. The base cabinet provides necessary storage. See Fig. 8-12. The components can be easily separated for rearranging or moving. A larger desk can easily be made with a second base unit and a longer top.

The desk features a typing shelf with metal side guides, which is useful for typing or as additional work space. See Fig. 8-13. The deep center drawer stores office supplies. The bottom file drawer is made to fit 9-by-12-inch file folders. The base unit could also be constructed with two large file drawers.

Begin construction by laying out sides of the base unit. See Table 8-3 (p. 319). Space crossmembers to fit the various sizes of drawers. See Fig. 8-14. Cut a ¼-by-¼-inch-deep rabbet along the back edge of the sides to receive the back. Cut ¾-by-⅜-inch-deep dado joints 3 inches in from the front and back for the crossmembers. Cut the notch for the toeboard. Make sure the sides are made in pairs.

Cut the crossmembers and toeboard for the base unit. Locate crossmembers in the joints and drill at a slight angle for screws. See Fig. 8-15 (p. 320). Assemble with glue and screws. Cut ¾-by-⅜-inch-deep rabbets in toeboard. Install the toeboard with glue and finish nails. Be sure the case is square as it is assembled. Machine facing and attach with glue and wire brads. Install metal side guides. Install back.

Cut material for the drawers. Make a ¼-by-¼-inch-deep groove for the bottom, on all pieces. Place ¼ inch up from the bottom edge. Cut a ½-by-¼-inch-deep rabbet on the ends of the sides. See Fig. 8-16. Cut and fit the bottom. Glue and assemble the drawers with finish nails.

Cut material for the decorative fronts. Locate the fronts with a ¾-inch overhang on both ends. They should be flush with the bottom. Drill and attach with screws from inside the drawer. Install metal side guides.

Fig. 8-13. Typing shelf with metal side guides.

Cut material for the typing shelf. Glue and clamp the top surface to the sides. Drill matching dowel holes to attach the front. Attach metal side guides. Note that all drawer fronts have a 45-degree bevel at the bottom edge to serve as a drawer pull. See Fig. 8-17.

Cut material for the top surface. Glue and nail into a 1½-inch-thick piece. Joint edges smooth. Cut and attach Formica, as discussed in Chapter 6. Attach leg brackets on one end 3½ inches in from each edge. Drill a large hole in the wood so that the leg bolt can be screwed in without binding.

Machine the legs to size. Drill for the leg bolt, and install. Installation is easy with two nuts locked against each other to turn

Table 8-3. Office Desk Material List
Dimensions are finished size.

Case

Sides	2 pc. ³⁄₄″ × 24³⁄₄″ × 28¹⁄₂″	Birch plywood
Crossmembers	8 pc. ³⁄₄″ × 2″ × 15¹⁄₂″	Birch plywood
Back	1 pc. ¹⁄₄″ × 15¹⁄₂″ × 28¹⁄₂″	Fir plywood
Facing	2 pc. ¹⁄₄″ × ³⁄₄″ × 25¹⁄₂″	Oak
	2 pc. ¹⁄₄″ × ³⁄₄″ × 14³⁄₄″	Oak
Toeboard	1 pc. ³⁄₄″ × 3″ × 16¹⁄₄″	Oak
Drawer guides	3 pr. 24″ metal side guides	

Top

Board	2 pc. ³⁄₄″ × 30″ × 48″	Fir plywood
Covering	1 pc. 48″ × 6′	Formica
Leg bracket	2 pc.	
Leg bolts	2 pc.	
Legs	2 pc. 1³⁄₄″ × 1³⁄₄″ × 28¹⁄₄″	Oak

Drawers

Sides	2 pc. ¹⁄₂″ × 10¹⁄₂″ × 24″	Birch plywood
	2 pc. ¹⁄₂″ × 7¹⁄₂″ × 24″	Birch plywood
Front, back	2 pc. ¹⁄₂″ × 10¹⁄₂″ × 13¹⁄₄″	Birch plywood
	2 pc. ¹⁄₂″ × 7¹⁄₂″ × 13¹⁄₄″	Birch plywood
Front trim	1 pc. ³⁄₄″ × 8³⁄₄″ × 15¹⁄₄″	Oak
	1 pc. ³⁄₄″ × 11″ × 15¹⁄₄″	Oak
Bottoms	2 pc. ¹⁄₄″ × 13¹⁄₄″ × 23¹⁄₂″	Fir plywood

Typing Shelf

Shelf	1 pc. ³⁄₄″ × 13³⁄₄″ × 24″	Birch plywood
Sides	2 pc. 1¹⁄₄″ × 2¹⁄₄″ × 24″	Spruce
Front	1 pc. ³⁄₄″ × 3¹⁄₂″ × 15¹⁄₄″	Oak

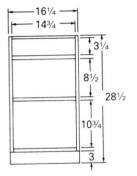
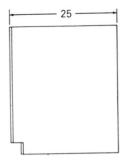

Fig. 8-14. Office desk base unit.

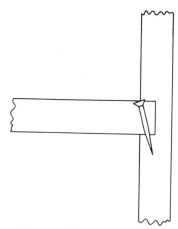

Fig. 8-15. Screw placement in crossmember.

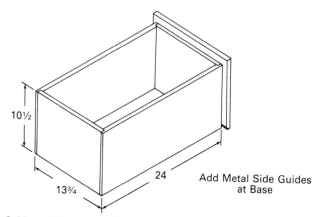

10½

13¾

24

Add Metal Side Guides
at Base

Fig. 8-16. Office desk file drawer.

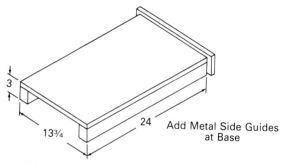

3

13¾

24

Add Metal Side Guides
at Base

Fig. 8-17. Office desk typing shelf.

with a wrench. Back off the nuts after secure penetration is reached. Install legs. Set top and legs on the base unit.

Finish with the desired stain and finish material.

Platform Bed

The platform bed is a very simple project. It is basically constructed as a plywood box with trim added to conceal the plywood edges. See Fig. 8-18. Birch plywood suitable for cabinetmaking works well, and can be stained to any color desired. If the bed is to be painted and used in a child's room, fir plywood can be used.

Begin construction by cutting plywood sides and ends. See Table 8-4 (p. 322). Cut a ¾-by-⅜-inch-deep rabbet along the top edge of each piece to receive the top surface. The ends will receive a ¾-by-⅜-inch-deep rabbet on each edge to receive the sides. Cut drawer openings in the front piece. Note that the side, top, and center spacing is 1½ inches and a 2-inch space is left at the bottom for bracing. Cut the top surface to size.

Begin assembly by gluing and nailing the corners of the box.

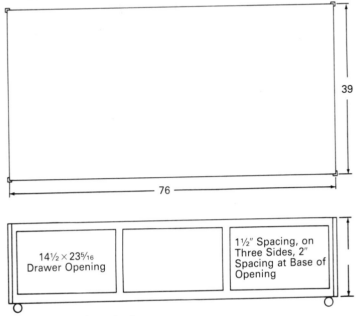

Fig. 8-18.   Platform bed.

Table 8-4. Platform Bed Material List
Dimensions are finished size.

Case		
Sides	2 pc. ¾″ × 18″ × 76″	Birch plywood
Ends	2 pc. ¾″ × 18″ × 38¼″	Birch plywood
Top	1 pc. ¾″ × 38¼″ × 75¼″	Fir plywood
Braces	2 pc. 1½″ × 1½″ × 75¼″	Spruce 2 × 4
Crossmembers	2 pc. 1½″ × 1½″ × 37½″	Spruce 2 × 4
End braces	2 pc. ¾″ × 1½″ × 37½″	Pine
Corner trim	4 pc. ¾″ × 1″ × 18″	Maple
Drawer guides	3 pr. 24″ metal side guides	
Drawers		
Sides	6 pc. ⅜″ × 14″ × 36″	Fir plywood
Front, back	6 pc. ⅜″ × 14″ × 21⅞″	Fir plywood
Bottom	3 pc. ⅜″ × 21⅞″ × 35⅝″	Fir plywood
Front trim	3 pc. ¾″ × 14¾″ × 23¾″	Birch plywood

Be sure all joints pull up tightly. Insert the top, use glue, and clamp with bar clamps. Insertion of the top will assure that the box is square.

Place the 2-by-2-inch braces along the lower edge of the box. Glue and clamp. See Fig. 8-19. These hold the weight of the drawers and provide a good attachment for the crossmembers. Place crossmembers at ends and between the drawers. Glue and clamp. Be sure middle crossmembers are square with the box and parallel to provide the desired drawer opening. Cut L-shaped trim from the ¾-by-1-inch pieces. Glue and clamp at the corners. Install metal side guides for drawers.

Cut ⅜-inch plywood material for the drawers. Make a ⅜-by-1/16-inch-deep groove at the bottom, on all pieces. Place ¼ inch up

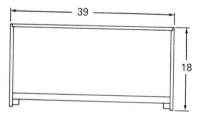

Braces Inside of Spruce 2 × 4's

Fig. 8-19. Platform bed, cross section.

from the bottom edge. Cut a ⅜-by-³/₁₆-inch-deep rabbet on the ends of the sides. See Fig. 8-20. Cut and fit the bottom. Glue and assemble the drawers with finish nails. Note that when metal side guides are used, the drawers must be 1 inch narrower than the opening provided.

Cut material for the decorative drawer fronts. Overall sizes of the fronts are given. Actual size will depend upon the type of trim used to cover the plywood edges (see Chapter 6). Complete the drawer fronts by using the router and core box bit to make a finger pull behind the base of each drawer front.

Center the drawer front on the drawer. It should be flush with the bottom. Drill and attach with screws from inside the drawer. Install the metal side guides.

Do the final sanding of all surfaces. Slightly round off all sharp corners. Finish with desired stain and finish material. See Fig. 8-21. The bed may be mounted on casters or placed permanently on a base of 2 by 4's.

Kitchen Cabinets, Base

The kitchen cabinet is intended as an example of construction methods. See Fig. 8-22. The basic structural components are side and center partitions. See Fig. 8-23. Various sizes of base cabinets can

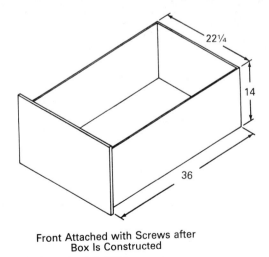

Front Attached with Screws after
Box Is Constructed

Fig. 8-20. **Platform bed drawer.**

Fig. 8-21. Finish platform bed with solid wood trim and casters.

be made by extending the length of the upper crossmembers and adding the necessary center partitions. This type of structure is strong and sturdy as compared to many commercial models. The cabinets can be easily made in the shop and later installed or transported in pieces and assembled on site. The cabinets may be finished with any desired type of door and drawer front.

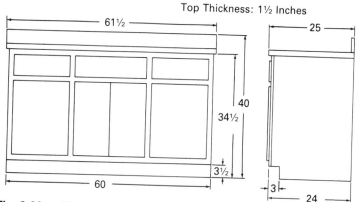

Fig. 8-22. Kitchen cabinet, lower.

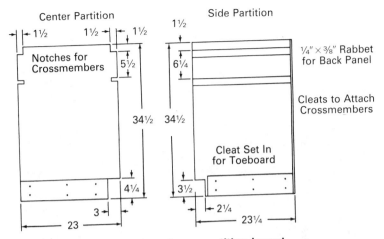

Fig. 8-23. Kitchen cabinet, lower partition layout.

Begin construction by laying out and cutting the side and center partitions. See Table 8-5 (p. 326). Cut a ⅜ × ¼-inch rabbet along the edge of the sides to receive the back. Remember to make the sides in pairs. Note that the center partitions are ¼ inch narrower to allow for back attachment. The notch for the toeboard is larger in the center partition to permit the board to extend through. Cut all notches with a saber saw or band saw.

Cut cleats to size from common pine. Glue and nail cleats in place. The base cleat is set back ¾ inch on the sides to receive the toeboard. Base cleats are flush on the center partitions.

Cut the bottom pieces, crossmembers, and toeboard to size. Begin assembly by gluing and nailing the bottoms in place. See Fig. 8-24. Glue and screw the crossmembers in place to strengthen the partitions, making sure that the skeleton is square. Install toeboard.

Cut face pieces to size and length. See Fig. 8-25. Locate all pieces in proper relation to each other and mark the edges. Use a dowel jig to drill the dowel holes. Drill with the front of the facing always in the same direction so the dowels will align when put together. Drill all holes ¾ inch deep. Use tape to mark the drill for depth. Cut dowels to length. Glue and clamp facing. Be sure that the structure pulls together square.

Drill facing to attach to the cabinet. Nail and glue to partitions and bottom shelves. Locate and install metal side guides in drawer openings. Install filler boards of the necessary thickness. Cut back panel and install.

Table 8-5. Kitchen Cabinet Material List (Lower Cabinet)
Dimensions are finished size.

Case		
Partitions	2 pc. ¾″ × 23¼″ × 34½″	Birch plywood
	2 pc. ¾″ × 23″ × 34½″	Fir plywood
Bottom	1 pc. ¾″ × 23″ × 22½″	Fir plywood
	2 pc. ¾″ × 23″ × 17¼″	Fir plywood
Cleats	6 pc. ¾″ × 4¼″ × 20″	Pine
	4 pc. ¾″ × 1½″ × 23″	Pine
Crossmembers	4 pc. ¾″ × 1½″ × 58½″	Pine
Toeboard	1 pc. ¾″ × 4¼″ × 58½″	Pine
Back panel	1 pc. ¼″ × 30¼″ × 59¼″	Fir plywood
Top		
Board	2 pc. ¾″ × 25″ × 61½″	Fir plywood
Backsplash	1 pc. ¾″ × 4″ × 61½″	Fir plywood
Covering	1 pc. 36″ × 8′	Formica
Screws	8 pc. 1½″ #8 flat head	
	6 pc. 2¼″ #8 flat head	
Facing		
Horizontal	3 pc. ¾″ × 1½″ × 57″	Birch
Vertical	2 pc. ¾″ × 1½″ × 31″	Birch
Between drawers	2 pc. ¾″ × 1½″ × 5½″	Birch
Between doors	2 pc. ¾″ × 1½″ × 21″	Birch
Drawers		
Sides	4 pc. ½″ × 5¼″ × 23″	Pine
Front, back	4 pc. ½″ × 5¼″ × 15″	Pine
Front trim	2 pc. ¾″ × 6″ × 17″	Birch
	1 pc. ¾″ × 6″ × 21½″	Birch
Bottom	2 pc. ¼″ × 15″ × 22½″	Fir plywood
Guides	2 pr. 20″ metal side guides	
Doors		
Fronts	2 pc. ¾″ × 17″ × 21½″	Birch plywood
	1 pc. ¾″ × 21½″ × 21½″	Birch plywood
Hardware		
Hinges	4 pr.	
Handles	6 pc.	

Cut pieces for drawers. The box-type drawer with decorative front is used in the kitchen cabinet. Check fit for 1-inch allowance for metal guides. Glue and nail drawers to assemble. Install second half of guide on the drawers.

Select the type of drawer fronts and doors. Fronts will be screwed to drawers. Hang doors with the appropriate hinges, pref-

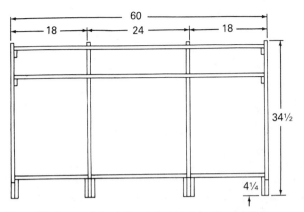

Fig. 8-24. Kitchen cabinet (lower) construction detail.

erably self-sprung hinges. Fronts should overlap facing ¼ inch on all edges.

Cut plywood for top and backsplash. Cut sink opening in the top piece. Use template provided with the sink. In the second top, cut sink opening ¾ inch larger all around. This will allow for easy clamping of self-rimming sinks. Glue and nail the tops to form a 1½-inch-thick surface.

Cut Formica to fit, with ¼ inch overlap on all edges. Be careful when cutting out sink opening and handling the piece. Carry out Formica work as shown in Chapter 6.

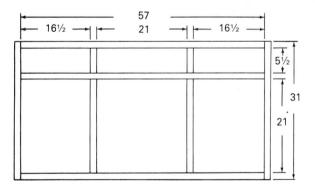

All Material ¾″ × 1½″ Square
Joints Doweled and Glued

Fig. 8-25. Kitchen cabinet, lower facing.

Drill for screws and attach backsplash. Place top flush with back and centered. Drill holes in crossmembers and attach with screws from underneath.

Finish cabinets with desired stain and finish material. Attach hardware.

Upper Kitchen Cabinets

The upper kitchen cabinets are made in the same decor as the base cabinets. They should be made the same overall length as the lower cabinets, with the side and center units also the same. See Fig. 8-26. The upper unit is intended as an example of construction methods.

The upper cabinets are made to specific standards, as are the lower cabinets. These are demonstrated in Chapter 2. Note that the upper cabinets allow an 18-inch clearance for a work area above the base cabinets. The upper cabinets then extend to the drop ceiling. Additional clearance is allowed above the sink. If a window is located in this area, a decorative valance is used to trim between cabinets.

Begin construction by laying out the side and center partitions. See Table 8-6 (p. 329). The sides are cut 11¾ inches wide for economical use of the plywood. The overall depth is 12½ inches, including facing. Cut a ¼-by-¼-inch-deep rabbet along the back edge of the sides to receive the backs. Cut ¾-by-¼-inch-deep dado joints for the shelves.

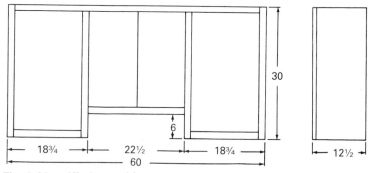

Fig. 8-26.   Kitchen cabinet, upper.

Table 8-6. Upper Kitchen Cabinet Material List
Dimensions are finished size.

Cabinet		
Sides	4 pc. ¾″ × 11¾″ × 30″	Birch plywood
Shelves	8 pc. ¾″ × 11½″ × 17¾″	Birch plywood
	3 pc. ¾″ × 11½″ × 23″	Birch plywood
Brace	2 pc. ¾″ × 3″ × 17¼″	Pine
Back	2 pc. ¼″ × 17¾″ × 29¼″	Fir plywood
	1 pc. ¼″ × 23″ × 23¼″	Fir plywood
Facing		
Horizontal	1 pc. ¾″ × 1½″ × 57″	Birch
	1 pc. ¾″ × 1½″ × 22½″	Birch
	2 pc. ¾″ × 1½″ × 15¾″	Birch
Vertical	2 pc. ¾″ × 1½″ × 30″	Birch
	2 pc. ¾″ × 1½″ × 28½″	Birch
Doors		
Ends	2 pc. ¾″ × 16¼″ × 27½″	Birch plywood
Middle	2 pc. ¾″ × 11½″ × 21½″	Birch plywood
Hardware		
Hinges	4 pr.	
Handles	4 pc.	

Cut all shelves to size. See Fig. 8-27. Note that the shelves are ¼ inch narrower to allow for the back. The lower shelf in each section is ¾ inch above the bottom so that it will be flush with the top of the lower facing.

Begin assembly by gluing and nailing the center section. Use

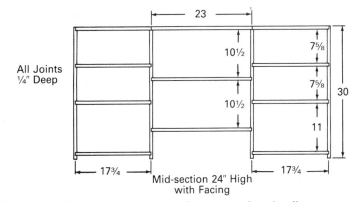

Fig. 8-27. Kitchen cabinet (upper) construction detail.

white glue and finish nails. When this section has dried, add the left and right sections. Be sure joints pull up tight and that the cabinet is square.

Cut face pieces to size and length. Locate all pieces in proper relation to each other and mark the edges. Use a dowel jig to drill the dowel holes. Drill with the front of the facing always in the same direction so the dowels will align when put together. Drill all holes ¾ inch deep. Use tape to mark the drill for depth. Cut dowels to length. Glue and clamp facing. Be sure that the structure pulls together square. Drill facing to attach to cabinet. Nail and glue to partitions and shelves.

Make door fronts to match the base cabinets. Finish with the desired stain and finish material.

Attach hardware.

Bathroom Vanity

A vanity is built as a box with a facing. See Fig. 8-28. The example shows how to fabricate the basic pieces. See Fig. 8-29. All such structures are composed of these parts. Any size of vanity may be built simply by extending the length. In Chapter 2 you will find suggested facing to accompany the various sizes. A ceramic or Formica top is added to finish the cabinet.

Various styles of doors and drawer fronts may be used. See Fig. 8-30. These should conform with the existing decor. The modern

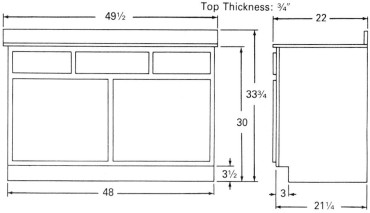

Fig. 8-28. Bathroom vanity.

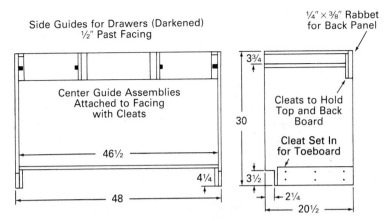

Side Guides for Drawers (Darkened)
½" Past Facing

¼" × ⅜" Rabbet
for Back Panel

Center Guide Assemblies
Attached to Facing
with Cleats

46½

48

4¼

3¾

30

Cleats to Hold
Top and Back
Board

Cleat Set In
for Toeboard

3½

2¼

20½

Fig. 8-29. Bathroom vanity, construction detail.

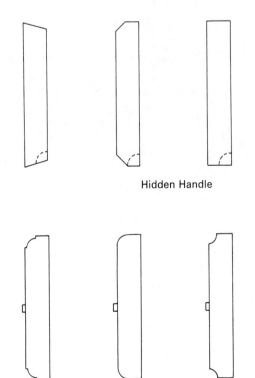

Hidden Handle

Fig. 8-30. Drawer front designs.

drawer fronts have matching plain doors. The drawer fronts with decorative edges may have matching plain or panel doors. The sample vanity has beveled edges on the drawer fronts. The matching plain doors have "V" grooves to simulate individual boards. See Fig. 8-31.

Begin construction by laying out and cutting the sides. See Table 8-7. Cut the notch for the toeboard. Cut the ⅜-by-¼-inch-deep rabbet along the back edge of each piece. Remember to make the sides in pairs.

Glue and nail cleats in place to hold the top and back board.

Fig. 8-31. **Bathroom vanity.**

Table 8-7. Vanity Material List
Dimensions are finished size.

Case		
Sides	2 pc. ¾″ × 20½″ × 30″	Birch plywood
Bottom	1 pc. ¾″ × 20¼″ × 46½″	Fir plywood
Cleats	2 pc. ¾″ × 4¼″ × 17¼″	Pine
Toeboard	1 pc. ¾″ × 4¼″ × 46½″	Pine
Back board	1 pc. ¾″ × 6″ × 46½″	Pine
Back panel	1 pc. ¼″ × 26″ × 47¼″	Fir plywood
Partitions	2 pc. ¾″ × 6″ × 19½″	Fir plywood
Drawer guides	2 pc. ¾″ × 1¼″ × 18¾″	Pine
	2 pc. ¾″ × ½″ × 18¾″	Pine
Cleats	2 pc. ¾″ × 1½″ × 19½″	Pine
	6 pc. ¾″ × 1½″ × 5″	Pine
Top		
Board	1 pc. ¾″ × 22″ × 49½″	Fir plywood
Backsplash	1 pc. ¾″ × 3″ × 49½″	Fir plywood
Covering	1 pc. 30″ × 10′	Formica
Screws	6 pc. 1½″ #8 flat head	
	6 pc. 1¼″ #8 flat head	
Facing		
Horizontal	3 pc. ¾″ × 1½″ × 45″	Birch
Vertical	2 pc. ¾″ × 1½″ × 26½″	Birch
Between drawers	2 pc. ¾″ × 1½″ × 5″	Birch
Between doors	1 pc. ¾″ × 1½″ × 17″	Birch
Dowel	12 pc. ⅜″ dia., 1¼″	Birch
Drawers		
Sides	4 pc. ¾″ × 4 ¾″ × 20″	Pine
Front, back	4 pc. ¾″ × 4 ¾″ × 12½″	Pine
Front trim	2 pc. ¾″ × 5½″ × 13 ¾″	Birch
	1 pc. ¾″ × 5½″ × 17″	Birch
Bottom	2 pc. ¼″ × 12½″ × 19½″	Fir plywood
Doors		
Fronts	2 pc. ¾″ × 23″ × 17½″	Birch plywood
Hardware		
Hinges	2 pr.	
Handles	4 pc.	

These should be predrilled for attachment of other parts. Attach the drawer runners on the sides also. Attach base cleat. Be sure it is set back ¾ inch to receive the toeboard.

Cut the base, toeboard, and back board to size. Begin assembly by gluing and nailing the baseboard in place. Glue and screw the back board in place to strengthen the sides. Install toeboard.

Cut face pieces to size and length. See Fig. 8-32. Locate all pieces in proper relation to each other and mark dowel location. Use a dowel jig to drill the dowel holes. Drill with the front of the facing always in the same direction so the dowels will align when put together. Drill all holes ¾ inch deep. Use tape to mark the drill for depth. Cut dowels to length. Glue and clamp facing. Be sure that the structure pulls together square.

Drill facing to attach to cabinet. Nail and glue to sides and base. Construct the center drawer guide assemblies. Glue to back board and facing with cleats.

Cut pieces for drawers. Assemble as shown in Chapter 6. The box-type drawer with decorative front is used in the vanity. Cut grooves for side guides so that the drawer will center in the 5-inch opening. Fit to guides previously installed in the cabinet.

Cut material for drawer fronts and doors. Use a "V" grooving bit in the router to bevel the edges and groove the doors. Attach the doors with self-sprung offset hinges. Overlap on all edges should be ¼ inch. Use screws to attach the decorative fronts to the drawers. Fronts should also have a ¼-inch overlap.

Cut plywood for top and backsplash. Cut the sink opening in the top piece. Use the template provided with the sink. Cut Formica to fit, with a ¼-inch overhang on all edges. Use care when cutting out the sink opening and handling the piece. Carry out Formica work as shown in Chapter 6.

Drill for screws and attach backsplash. Place top flush with

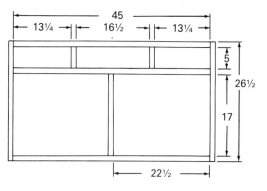

All Material 3/4″ × 1½″ Square

Joints Doweled and Glued

Fig. 8-32.   Bathroom vanity facing.

back and centered. Screw in place from underneath. Attach ¼-inch-thick plywood back.

The vanity has been finished with stain that seals the wood.

Cubes

These cubes have been designed to allow maximum versatility in use. A group of cubes can be easily arranged for various purposes. See Fig. 8-33. These work well in bedrooms as shelving or chests, in the living or recreation room for storage or display purposes. With partitions added they more closely fit the needs of a music center. See Fig. 8-34. With drawers or doors attached to the front, the cubes become a true cabinet.

The cubes are best constructed of birch plywood. See Table 8-8 (p. 336). This makes finishing, whether staining or painting, a much easier and rewarding job. Begin by ripping the plywood sheet to 19⅝ inches wide. Add an allowance to smooth edges on the jointer. Crosscut to exact length for sides, top, and bottom. Cut the 20-inch-wide back from the remaining piece. Follow the same procedure to square up the piece.

Cut the joints after all parts have been cut to exact sizes and

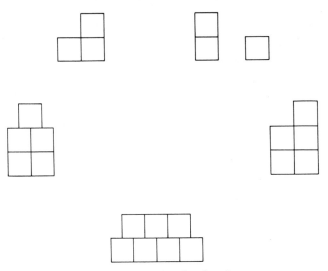

Fig. 8-33.   Possible arrangements of cube storage cases.

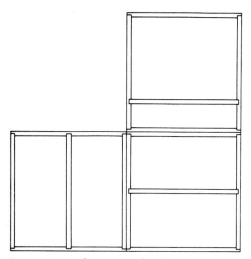

Fig. 8-34.   Arrangement for use as bookcase or music center.

square. See Fig. 8-35. Cut rabbet joints ¾ by ⅜ inch deep. This can be done with a router, table saw, or radial arm saw. Carry out a trial run for assembly without glue. Make sure the back fits easily in the opening. Any additional shelves or partitions also need to drop in easily. These may be made of ¾- or ½-inch-thick birch plywood.

Assembly can easily be carried out with finish nails. Put together the four sides of the box, glue, and nail. Install the back quickly; this will ensure the squareness of the box. After gluing and nailing, set the nails below the surface and fill the holes.

Sand all surfaces carefully. Use abrasive paper with a sanding block to keep all corners square. Sand all areas flush and slightly round off all corners. The front edges may be covered with com-

Table 8-8.   Cubes Material List
Dimensions are finished size

Box		
Sides	2 pc. ¾″ × 19⅝″ × 19¼″	Birch plywood
Top, bottom	2 pc. ¾″ × 19⅝″ × 20″	Birch plywood
Back	1 pc. ¾″ × 20″ × 20″	Birch plywood
Optional shelves	¾″ × 19¼″ × 19¼″	Birch plywood

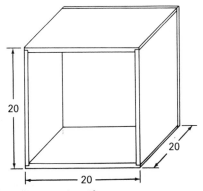

Fig. 8-35.   Basic cube construction.

mercial hardwood banding, if desired. The birch plywood edges should sand to provide an attractive edge.

Finish with stain and Danish oil finishes, or paint for accent. Remember to undercoat before painting. Cubes may also be covered with plastic laminate and used separately for tables.

Glossary

A-C exterior plywood: A sanded exterior panel grade described by face grade (A) and back (C) veneers bonded with exterior glue; used in siding, soffits, fences. Face is finish grade, and can be painted or stained.

A-D interior plywood: A sanded interior panel grade described by face grade (A) and back (D) veneers bonded with interior or exterior glue, used in cabinetwork. Face is finished grade, and can be painted or stained.

Annual rings: Concentric rings seen in the cross section of a tree, caused by its yearly growth.

Bench stop: A device placed in a hole in the bench surface so that material can be clamped between it and the vise dog.

Cleat: A square wood piece, usually ¾ by ¾ inch, used with glue and screws to hold adjacent cabinet parts at a right angle.

Conifer: Evergreen, cone-bearing trees, such as pine, spruce, and fir.

Deciduous: Trees that shed their leaves annually, typically hardwoods, such as cherry, maple, and oak.

Doors, panel: A door made with a solid wood frame, connected with dowels or tenons. A center panel may be flat or raised.

Doors, plain: A flat door, usually made of plywood. Edges are beveled or covered with square trim.

Dowel jig: A device used to align matching holes for dowel joints. Often a homemade wooden device will perform this function.

Edge: The long surface of a board that is both perpendicular and parallel to the face surface.

Edging: Solid wood pieces, from ¼ inch to ¾ inch thick, nailed and glued on the edge of plywood to conceal the veneer layers.

End: The surface of the board that shows the growth rings of the tree.

Facing: A structure usually made of ¾-inch-thick stock, doweled together, and glued and nailed to the front of a cabinet. This provides the openings for drawers and doors.

339

Hardwood: Wood typically from a broad-leafed tree, such as maple, cherry, or oak.

Jointing: To generate a flat and true surface on the jointer.

Lay out: To place lines on the surface of a board for cutting or drilling.

Longitudinal: The long axis of a tree or board that is parallel to the direction of the grain.

Moisture equilibrium: Moisture in the wood in balance with the humidity in the air.

Radial: A plane or surface that radiates out from the center of the tree to form a lengthwise section.

Registration edge: A flat and true surface that is both perpendicular and parallel to the registration surface, used to square other surfaces.

Registration surface: A flat and true surface used to square all other surfaces: the second face, edges, and ends.

Softwood: Wood typically from a needle-bearing tree, such as pine, spruce, or fir.

Solid wood construction: Cabinetmaking projects made with boards as cut from the tree, in contrast to veneered construction.

Surface: The large, flat area of a piece of wood.

Surface (face): The surface of a board that is most beautiful and closest to being flat and true.

Surfacing: To generate a flat and true surface on the surfacer or planer that is parallel to the first surface.

Tangential: The surface of a board that is tangent to the annual rings.

Trim: Solid wood pieces glued on the edge of plywood to conceal the veneer layers. Usually wide enough to be shaped.

Veneer: Thin wood that has been peeled or sliced from a log, used as layers in making of plywood.

Veneered construction: Cabinetmaking projects made with plywood for the major parts.

Index

A

Air dried wood, 9–11
Aliphatic glues, 202
Aluminum level, 89, 93
Annual ring patterns, 6
Appearance (design), 63–66
  balance, 65
  emphasis, 66
  furniture style, 63
  harmony, 65
  proportion, 63–65
  rhythm, 65–66
Apron pieces, 230
Awls, 89, 93
Assembly tools, 109–13
  bar clamp, 109, 111
  claw hammer, 109
  corner clamp, 109, 112–13
  nail set, 109, 110
  screwdriver, 109, 110
  spring clamp, 109, 111
  web clamp, 109, 112
  wonder bar, 109, 110
Auger bit, 106, 108

B

Back saw, 93, 95
Band saw, 143–50
  circles with, 147–50
  compound cutting, 147
  cutting operations with, 144–47
  duplicate shapes, 150
  nibble cuts, 144
  parts of, 143–44
  relief cuts, 144
  resawing, 147
  tangent cuts, 144–47
  uses for, 143
Bar clamp, 109, 111, 178
  See also Clamping
Basic construction, 169–276
  cabinets, 212–34
  cutting to finished size, 183–84
  cutting to rough size, 171–75
  doors, 239–53
  drawers, 253–63
  fasteners, 264–74
  finishing, 274–76
  gluing up stock, 176–82
  joints, 184–203
  laying out rough sizes, 169–71
  plastic laminates, 235–39
  preparation for finishing, 272–74
  tables, 204–12
  veneered plywood and, 176
Bathroom vanity, 217–25, 330–35
  as project, 330–35
Bayonet saw. *See* Saber saw
Beds. *See* Platform beds

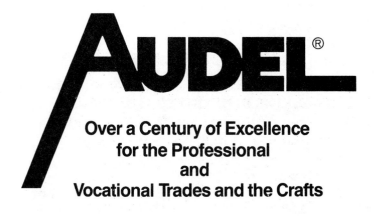

**Over a Century of Excellence
for the Professional
and
Vocational Trades and the Crafts**

**Order now from your local bookstore
or use the convenient order form at
the back of this book.**

AUDEL

These fully illustrated, up-to-date guides and manuals mean a better job done for mechanics, engineers, electricians, plumbers, carpenters, and all skilled workers.

Contents

Electrical

House Wiring sixth edition
Roland E. Palmquist
5½ x 8¼ Hardcover 256 pp. 150 illus.
ISBN: 0-672-23404-1 $13.95

Rules and regulations of the current National Electrical Code® for residential wiring, fully explained and illustrated: • basis for load calculations • calculations for dwellings • services • nonmetallic-sheathed cable • underground feeder and branch-circuit cable • metal-clad cable • circuits required for dwellings • boxes and fittings • receptacle spacing • mobile homes • wiring for electric house heating.

Practical Electricity fourth edition
Robert G. Middleton; revised by L. Donald Meyers
5½ x 8¼ Hardcover 504 pp. 335 illus.
ISBN: 0-672-23375-4 $14.95

Complete, concise handbook on the principles of electricity and their practical application: • magnetism and electricity • conductors and insulators • circuits • electromagnetic induction • alternating current • electric lighting and lighting calculations • basic house wiring • electric heating • generating stations and substations.

Guide to the 1984 Electrical Code®
Roland E. Palmquist
5½ × 8¼ Hardcover 664 pp. 225 illus.
ISBN: 0-672-23398-3 $19.95

Authoritative guide to the National Electrical Code® for all electricians, contractors, inspectors, and homeowners: • terms and regulations for wiring design and protection • wiring methods and materials • equipment for general use • special occupancies • special equipment and conditions • and communication systems. Guide to the 1987 NEC® will be available in mid-1987.

Mathematics for Electricians and Electronics Technicians
Rex Miller
5½ x 8¼ Hardcover 312 pp. 115 illus.
ISBN: 0-8161-1700-4 $14.95

Mathematical concepts, formulas, and problem solving in electricity and electronics: • resistors and resistance • circuits • meters • alternating current and inductance • alternating current and capacitance • impedance and phase angles • resonance in circuits • special-purpose circuits. Includes mathematical problems and solutions.

Fractional Horsepower Electric Motors
Rex Miller and Mark Richard Miller
5½ x 8¼ Hardcover 436 pp. 285 illus.
ISBN: 0-672-23410-6 $15.95

Fully illustrated guide to small-to-moderate-size electric motors in home appliances and industrial equipment: • terminology • repair tools and supplies • small DC and universal motors • split-phase, capacitor-start, shaded pole, and special motors • commutators and brushes • shafts and bearings • switches and relays • armatures • stators • modification and replacement of motors.

Electric Motors
Edwin P. Anderson; revised by Rex Miller
5½ x 8¼ Hardcover 656 pp. 405 illus.
ISBN: 0-672-23376-2 $14.95

Complete guide to installation, maintenance, and repair of all types of electric motors: • AC generators • synchronous motors • squirrel-cage motors • wound rotor motors • DC motors • fractional-horsepower motors • magnetic contractors • motor testing and maintenance • motor calculations • meters • wiring diagrams • armature windings • DC armature rewinding procedure • and stator and coil winding.

Home Appliance Servicing fourth edition
Edwin P. Anderson; revised by Rex Miller
5½ x 8¼ Hardcover 640 pp. 345 illus.
ISBN: 0-672-23379-7 $15.95

Step-by-step illustrated instruction on all types of household appliances: • irons • toasters • roasters and broilers • electric coffee makers • space heaters • water heaters • electric ranges and microwave ovens • mixers and blenders • fans and blowers • vacuum cleaners and floor polishers • washers and dryers • dishwashers and garbage disposals • refrigerators • air conditioners and dehumidifiers.

Television Service Manual

fifth edition
Robert G. Middleton; revised by Joseph G. Barrile
5½ x 8¼   Hardcover   512 pp.   395 illus.
ISBN: 0-672-23395-9 $15.95

Practical up-to-date guide to all aspects of television transmission and reception, for both black and white and color receivers: • step-by-step maintenance and repair • broadcasting • transmission • receivers • antennas and transmission lines • interference • RF tuners • the video channel • circuits • power supplies • alignment • test equipment.

Electrical Course for Apprentices and Journeymen

second edition
Roland E. Palmquist
5½ x 8¼   Hardcover   478 pp.   290 illus.
ISBN:0-672-23393-2 $14.95

Practical course on operational theory and applications for training and re-training in school or on the job: • electricity and matter • units and definitions • electrical symbols • magnets and magnetic fields • capacitors • resistance • electromagnetism • instruments and measurements • alternating currents • DC generators • circuits • transformers • motors • grounding and ground testing.

Questions and Answers for Electricians Examinations eighth edition

Roland E. Palmquist
5½ x 8¼   Hardcover   320 pp.   110 illus.
ISBN: 0-672-23399-1 $12.95

Based on the current National Electrical Code®, a review of exams for apprentice, journeyman, and master, with explanations of principles underlying each test subject: • Ohm's Law and other formulas • power and power factors • lighting • branch circuits and feeders • transformer principles and connections • wiring • batteries and rectification • voltage generation • motors • ground and ground testing.

Machine Shop and Mechanical Trades

Machinists Library

fourth edition   3 vols
Rex Miller
5½ x 8¼   Hardcover   1,352 pp.   1,120 illus.
ISBN: 0-672-23380-0 $38.95

Indispensable three-volume reference for machinists, tool and die makers, machine operators, metal workers, and those with home workshops.

Volume I, Basic Machine Shop
5½ x 8¼   Hardcover   392 pp.   375 illus.
ISBN: 0-672-23381-9 $14.95

• Blueprint reading • benchwork • layout and measurement • sheet-metal hand tools and machines • cutting tools • drills • reamers • taps • threading dies • milling machine cutters, arbors, collets, and adapters.

Volume II, Machine Shop
5½ x 8¼   Hardcover 528 pp. 445 illus
ISBN: 0-672-23382-7 $14.95

• Power saws • machine tool operations • drilling machines • boring • lathes • automatic screw machine • milling • metal spinning.

Volume III, Toolmakers Handy Book
5½ x 8¼   Hardcover   432 pp.   300 illus.
ISBN: 0-672-23383-5 $14.95

• Layout work • jigs and fixtures • gears and gear cutting • dies and diemaking • toolmaking operations • heat-treating furnaces • induction heating • furnace brazing • cold-treating process.

Mathematics for Mechanical Technicians and Technologists

John D. Bies
5½ x 8¼   Hardcover 392 pp.   190 illus.
ISBN: 0-02-510620-1 $17.95

Practical sourcebook of concepts, formulas, and problem solving in industrial and mechanical technology: • basic and complex mechanics • strength of materials • fluidics • cams and gears • machine elements • machining operations • management controls • economics in machining • facility and human resources management.

Millwrights and Mechanics Guide

third edition
Carl A. Nelson
5½ x 8¼   Hardcover   1,040 pp.   880 illus.
ISBN: 0-672-23373-8 $22.95

Most comprehensive and authoritative guide available for millwrights and mechanics at all levels of work or supervision: • drawing and sketching

---

• machinery and equipment installation • principles of mechanical power transmission • V-belt drives • flat belts • gears • chain drives • couplings • bearings • structural steel • screw threads • mechanical fasteners • pipe fittings and valves • carpentry • sheet-metal work • blacksmithing • rigging • electricity • welding • pumps • portable power tools • mensuration and mechanical calculations.

Welders Guide third edition

James E. Brumbaugh
5½ x 8 ¼   Hardcover   960 pp.   615 illus.
ISBN: 0-672-23374-6 $23.95

Practical, concise manual on theory, operation, and maintenance of all welding machines: • gas welding equipment, supplies, and process • arc welding equipment, supplies, and process • TIG and MIG welding • submerged-arc and other shielded-arc welding processes • resistance, thermit, and stud welding • solders and soldering • brazing and braze welding • welding plastics • safety and health measures • symbols and definitions • testing and inspecting welds. Terminology and definitions as standardized by American Welding Society.

Welder/Fitters Guide

John P. Stewart
8½ x 11   Paperback   160 pp.   195 illus.
ISBN: 0-672-23325-8 $7.95

Step-by-step instruction for welder/fitters during training or on the job: • basic assembly tools and aids • improving blueprint reading skills • marking and alignment techniques • using basic tools • simple work practices • guide to fabricating welds • avoiding mistakes • exercises in blueprint reading • clamping devices • introduction to using hydraulic jacks • safety in weld fabrication plants • common welding shop terms.

Sheet Metal Work

John D. Bies
5½ x 8¼   Hardcover   456 pp.   215 illus.
ISBN: 0-8161-1706-3 $17.95

On-the-job sheet metal guide for manufacturing, construction, and home workshops: • mathematics for sheet metal work • principles of drafting • concepts of sheet metal drawing • sheet metal standards, specifications, and materials • safety practices • layout • shear cutting • holes • bending and folding • forming operations • notching and clipping • metal spinning • mechanical fastening • soldering and brazing • welding • surface preparation and finishes • production processes.

III

Power Plant Engineers Guide

third edition
Frank D. Graham; revised by Charlie Buffington
5¹/2 x 8¹/4 Hardcover 960 pp. 530 illus.
ISBN: 0-672-23329-0 $16.95

All-inclusive question-and-answer guide to steam and diesel-power engines: • fuels • heat • combustion • types of boilers • shell or fire-tube boiler construction • strength of boiler materials • boiler calculations • boiler fixtures, fittings, and attachments • boiler feed pumps • condensers • cooling ponds and cooling towers • boiler installation, startup, operation, maintenance and repair • oil, gas, and waste-fuel burners • steam turbines • air compressors • plant safety.

Mechanical Trades Pocket Manual

second edition
Carl A. Nelson
4 × 6 Paperback 364 pp. 255 illus.
ISBN: 0-672-23378-9 $10.95

Comprehensive handbook of essentials, pocket-sized to fit in the tool box: • mechanical and isometric drawing • machinery installation and assembly • belts • drives • gears • couplings • screw threads • mechanical fasteners • packing and seals • bearings • portable power tools • welding • rigging • piping • automatic sprinkler systems • carpentry • stair layout • electricity • shop geometry and trigonometry.

Plumbing

Plumbers and Pipe Fitters Library

third edition 3 vols
Charles N. McConnell; revised by Tom Philbin
5¹/2x8¹/4 Hardcover 952 pp. 560 illus.
ISBN: 0-672-23384-3 $34.95

Comprehensive three-volume set with up-to-date information for master plumbers, journeymen, apprentices, engineers, and those in building trades.

Volume 1, Materials, Tools, Roughing-In
5¹/2 x 8¹/4 Hardcover 304 pp. 240 illus.
ISBN: 0-672-23385-1 $12.95

• Materials • tools • pipe fitting • pipe joints • blueprints • fixtures • valves and faucets.

Volume 2, Welding, Heating, Air Conditioning
5¹/2 x 8¹/4 Hardcover 384 pp. 220 illus.
ISBN: 0-672-23386-X $13.95

• Brazing and welding • planning a

heating system • steam heating systems • hot water heating systems • boiler fittings • fuel-oil tank installation • gas piping • air conditioning.

Volume 3, Water Supply, Drainage, Calculations
5¹/2 x 8¹/4 Hardcover 264 pp. 100 illus.
ISBN: 0-672-23387-8 $12.95

• Drainage and venting • sewage disposal • soldering • lead work • mathematics and physics for plumbers and pipe fitters.

Home Plumbing Handbook third edition

Charles N. McConnell
8¹/2 x 11 Paperback 200 pp. 100 illus.
ISBN: 0-672-23413-0 $10.95

Clear, concise, up-to-date fully illustrated guide to home plumbing installation and repair: • repairing and replacing faucets • repairing toilet tanks • repairing a trip-lever bath drain • dealing with stopped-up drains • working with copper tubing • measuring and cutting pipe • PVC and CPVC pipe and fittings • installing a garbage disposals • replacing dishwashers • repairing and replacing water heaters • installing or resetting toilets • caulking around plumbing fixtures and tile • water conditioning • working with cast-iron soil pipe • septic tanks and disposal fields • private water systems.

The Plumbers Handbook seventh edition

Joseph P. Almond, Sr.
4 × 6 Paperback 352 pp. 170 illus.
ISBN: 0-672-23419-x $10.95

Comprehensive, handy guide for plumbers, pipe fitters, and apprentices that fits in the tool box or pocket: • plumbing tools • how to read blueprints • heating systems • water supply • fixtures, valves, and fittings • working drawings • roughing and repair • outside sewage lift station • pipes and pipelines • vents, drain lines, and septic systems • lead work • silver brazing and soft soldering • plumbing systems • abbreviations, definitions, symbols, and formulas.

Questions and Answers for Plumbers Examinations second edition

Jules Oravetz
5¹/2 x 8¹/4 Paperback 256 pp. 145 illus.
ISBN: 0-8161-1703-9 $9.95

Practical, fully illustrated study guide to licensing exams for apprentice, journeyman, or master plumber: • definitions, specifications, and regulations set by National Bureau of Standards and by various state codes

• basic plumbing installation • drawings and typical plumbing system layout • mathematics • materials and fittings • joints and connections • traps, cleanouts, and backwater valves • fixtures • drainage, vents, and vent piping • water supply and distribution • plastic pipe and fittings • steam and hot water heating.

HVAC

Air Conditioning: Home and Commercial second edition

Edwin P. Anderson; revised by Rex Miller
5¹/2 x 8¹/4 Hardcover 528 pp. 180 illus.
ISBN: 0-672-23397-5 $15.95

Complete guide to construction, installation, operation, maintenance, and repair of home, commercial, and industrial air conditioning systems, with troubleshooting charts: • heat leakage • ventilation requirements • room air conditioners • refrigerants • compressors • condensing equipment • evaporators • water-cooling systems • central air conditioning • automobile air conditioning • motors and motor control.

Heating, Ventilating and Air Conditioning Library second edition 3 vols

James E. Brumbaugh
5¹/2 x 8¹/4 Hardcover 1,840 pp. 1,275 illus.
ISBN: 0-672-23388-6 $42.95

Authoritative three-volume reference for those who install, operate, maintain, and repair HVAC equipment commercially, industrially, or at home. Each volume fully illustrated with photographs, drawings, tables and charts.

Volume I, Heating Fundamentals, Furnaces, Boilers, Boiler Conversions
5¹/2 x 8¹/4 Hardcover 656 pp. 405 illus.
ISBN: 0-672-23389-4 $16.95

• Insulation principles • heating calculations • fuels • warm-air, hot water, steam, and electrical heating systems • gas-fired, oil-fired, coal-fired, and electric-fired furnaces • boilers and boiler fittings • boiler and furnace conversion.

Volume II, Oil, Gas and Coal Burners, Controls, Ducts, Piping, Valves
5¹/2 x 8¹/4 Hardcover 592 pp. 455 illus.
ISBN: 0-672-23390-8 $15.95

• Coal firing methods • thermostats and humidistats • gas and oil controls and other automatic controls •

ducts and duct systems • pipes, pipe fittings, and piping details • valves and valve installation • steam and hot-water line controls.

Volume III, Radiant Heating, Water Heaters, Ventilation, Air Conditioning, Heat Pumps, Air Cleaners
5 1/2 x 8 1/4 Hardcover 592 pp. 415 illus.
ISBN: 0-672-23391-6 $14.95

• Radiators, convectors, and unit heaters • fireplaces, stoves, and chimneys • ventilation principles • fan selection and operation • air conditioning equipment • humidifiers and dehumidifiers • air cleaners and filters.

Oil Burners fourth edition
Edwin M. Field
5 1/2 x 8 1/4 Hardcover 360 pp. 170 illus.
ISBN: 0-672-23394-0 $15.95

Up-to-date sourcebook on the construction, installation, operation, testing, servicing, and repair of all types of oil burners, both industrial and domestic: • general electrical hookup and wiring diagrams of automatic control systems • ignition system • high-voltage transportation • operational sequence of limit controls, thermostats, and various relays • combustion chambers • drafts • chimneys • drive couplings • fans or blowers • burner nozzles • fuel pumps.

Refrigeration: Home and Commercial second edition
Edwin P. Anderson; revised by Rex Miller
5 1/2 x 8 1/4 Hardcover 768 pp. 285 illus.
ISBN: 0-672-23396-7 $17.95

Practical, comprehensive reference for technicians, plant engineers, and homeowners on the installation, operation, servicing, and repair of everything from single refrigeration units to commercial and industrial systems: • refrigerants • compressors • thermoelectric cooling • service equipment and tools • cabinet maintenance and repairs • compressor lubrication systems • brine systems • supermarket and grocery refrigeration • locker plants • fans and blowers • piping • heat leakage • refrigeration-load calculations.

Hydraulics for Off-the-Road Equipment second edition
Harry L. Stewart; revised by Tom Philbin
5 1/2 x 8 1/4 Hardcover 256 pp. 175 illus.
ISBN: 0-8161-1701-2 $13.95

Complete reference manual for those who own and operate heavy equipment and for engineers, designers, installation and maintenance technicians, and shop mechanics: • hydraulic pumps, accumulators, and motors • force components • hydraulic control components • filters and filtration, lines and fittings, and fluids • hydrostatic transmissions • maintenance • troubleshooting.

Pneumatics and Hydraulics fourth edition
Harry L. Stewart; revised by Tom Philbin
5 1/2 x 8 1/4 Hardcover 512 pp. 315 illus.
ISBN: 0-672-23412-2 $15.95

Practical guide to the principles and applications of fluid power for engineers, designers, process planners, tool men, shop foremen, and mechanics: • pressure, work and power • general features of machines • hydraulic and pneumatic symbols • pressure boosters • air compressors and accessories • hydraulic power devices • hydraulic fluids • piping • air filters, pressure regulators, and lubricators • flow and pressure controls • pneumatic motors and tools • rotary hydraulic motors and hydraulic transmissions • pneumatic circuits • hydraulic circuits • servo systems.

Pumps fourth edition
Harry L. Stewart; revised by Tom Philbin
5 1/2 x 8 1/4 Hardcover 508 pp. 360 illus.
ISBN: 0-672-23400-9 $15.95

Comprehensive guide for operators, engineers, maintenance workers, inspectors, superintendents, and mechanics on principles and day-to-day operations of pumps: • centrifugal, rotary, reciprocating, and special service pumps • hydraulic accumulators • power transmission • hydraulic power tools • hydraulic cylinders • control valves • hydraulic fluids • fluid lines and fittings.

Carpenters and Builders Library
fifth edition
John E. Ball; revised by Tom Philbin
5 1/2 x 8 1/4 Hardcover 1,224 pp. 1,010 illus.
ISBN: 0-672-23369-x $39.95
Also available in a new boxed set at no extra cost:
ISBN: 0-02-506450-9 $39.95

These profusely illustrated volumes, available in a handsome boxed edition, have set the professional standard for carpenters, joiners, and woodworkers.

Volume 1, Tools, Steel Square, Joinery
5 1/2 x 8 1/4 Hardcover 384 pp. 345 illus.
ISBN: 0-672-23365-7 $10.95

• Woods • nails • screws • bolts • the workbench • tools • using the steel square • joints and joinery • cabinetmaking joints • wood patternmaking • and kitchen cabinet construction.

Volume 2, Builders Math, Plans, Specifications
5 1/2 x 8 1/4 Hardcover 304 pp. 205 illus.
ISBN: 0-672-23366-5 $10.95

• Surveying • strength of timbers • practical drawing • architectural drawing • barn construction • small house construction • and home workshop layout.

Volume 3, Layouts, Foundations, Framing
5 1/2 x 8 1/4 Hardcover 272 pp. 215 illus.
ISBN: 0-672-23367-3 $10.95

• Foundations • concrete forms • concrete block construction • framing, girders and sills • skylights • porches and patios • chimneys, fireplaces, and stoves • insulation • solar energy and paneling.

Volume 4, Millwork, Power Tools, Painting
5 1/2 x 8 1/4 Hardcover 344 pp. 245 illus.
ISBN: 0-672-23368-1 $10.95

• Roofing, miter work • doors • windows, sheathing and siding • stairs • flooring • table saws, band saws, and jigsaws • wood lathes • sanders and combination tools • portable power tools • painting.

Complete Building Construction
second edition
John Phelps; revised by Tom Philbin
5 1/2 x 8 1/4 Hardcover 744 pp. 645 illus.
ISBN: 0-672-23377-0 $19.95

Comprehensive guide to constructing a frame or brick building from the footings to the ridge: • laying out building and excavation lines • making concrete forms and pouring fittings and foundation • making concrete slabs, walks, and driveways • laying concrete block, brick, and tile • building chimneys and fireplaces • framing, siding, and roofing • insulating • finishing the inside • building stairs • installing windows • hanging doors.

Complete Roofing Handbook
James E. Brumbaugh
5¹/₂ x 8¹/₄   Hardcover 536 pp.   510 illus.
ISBN: 0-02-517850-4 $29.95

Authoritative text and highly detailed drawings and photographs,on all aspects of roofing: • types of roofs • roofing and reroofing • roof and attic insulation and ventilation • skylights and roof openings • dormer construction • roof flashing details • shingles • roll roofing • built-up roofing • roofing with wood shingles and shakes • slate and tile roofing • installing gutters and downspouts • listings of professional and trade associations and roofing manufacturers.

Complete Siding Handbook
James E. Brumbaugh
5¹/₂ x 8¹/₄   Hardcover 512 pp.   450 illus.
ISBN: 0-02-517880-6 $23.95

Companion to *Complete Roofing Handbook*, with step-by-step instructions and drawings on every aspect of siding: • sidewalls and siding • wall preparation • wood board siding • plywood panel and lap siding • hardboard panel and lap siding • wood shingle and shake siding • aluminum and steel siding • vinyl siding • exterior paints and stains • refinishing of siding, gutter and downspout systems • listings of professional and trade associations and siding manufacturers.

Masons and Builders Library
second edition   2 vols
Louis M. Dezettel; revised by Tom Philbin
5¹/₂ x 8¹/₄   Hardcover 688 pp.   500 illus.
ISBN: 0-672-23401-7 $23.95

Two-volume set on practical instruction in all aspects of materials and methods of bricklaying and masonry: • brick • mortar • tools • bonding • corners, openings, and arches • chimneys and fireplaces • structural clay tile and glass block • brick walks, floors, and terraces • repair and maintenance • plasterboard and plaster • stone and rock masonry • reading blueprints.

Volume 1, Concrete, Block, Tile, Terrazzo
5¹/₂ x 8¹/₄   Hardcover 304 pp.   190 illus.
ISBN: 0-672-23402-5 $13.95

Volume 2, Bricklaying, Plastering, Rock Masonry, Clay Tile
5¹/₂ x 8¹/₄   Hardcover 384 pp.   310 illus.
ISBN: 0-672-23403-3 $12.95

Woodworking

Woodworking and Cabinetmaking
F. Richard Boller
5¹/₂ x 8¹/₄   Hardcover 360 pp.   455 illus.
ISBN: 0-02-512800-0 $16.95

Compact one-volume guide to the essentials of all aspects of woodworking: • properties of softwoods, hardwoods, plywood, and composition wood • design, function, appearance, and structure • project planning • hand tools • machines • portable electric tools • construction • the home workshop • and the projects themselves – stereo cabinet, speaker cabinets, bookcase, desk, platform bed, kitchen cabinets, bathroom vanity.

Wood Furniture: Finishing, Refinishing, Repairing second edition
James E. Brumbaugh
5¹/₂ x 8¹/₄   Hardcover 352 pp.   185 illus.
ISBN: 0-672-23409-2 $12.95

Complete, fully illustrated guide to repairing furniture and to finishing and refinishing wood surfaces for professional woodworkers and do-it-yourselfers: • tools and supplies • types of wood • veneering • inlaying • repairing, restoring, and stripping • wood preparation • staining • shellac, varnish, lacquer, paint and enamel, and oil and wax finishes • antiquing • gilding and bronzing • decorating furniture.

Maintenance and Repair

Building Maintenance second edition
Jules Oravetz
5¹/₂ x 8¹/₄   Hardcover 384 pp.   210 illus.
ISBN: 0-672-23278-2 $9.95

Complete information on professional maintenance procedures used in office, educational, and commercial buildings: • painting and decorating • plumbing and pipe fitting

• concrete and masonry • carpentry • roofing • glazing and caulking • sheet metal • electricity • air conditioning and refrigeration • insect and rodent control • heating • maintenance management • custodial practices.

Gardening, Landscaping and Grounds Maintenance
third edition
Jules Oravetz
5¹/₂ x 8¹/₄   Hardcover 424 pp.   340 illus.
ISBN: 0-672-23417-3 $15.95

Practical information for those who maintain lawns, gardens, and industrial, municipal, and estate grounds: • flowers, vegetables, berries, and house plants • greenhouses • lawns • hedges and vines • flowering shrubs and trees • shade, fruit and nut trees • evergreens • bird sanctuaries • fences • insect and rodent control • weed and brush control • roads, walks, and pavements • drainage • maintenance equipment • golf course planning and maintenance.

Home Maintenance and Repair: Walls, Ceilings and Floors
Gary D. Branson
8¹/₂ x 11   Paperback 80 pp.   80 illus.
ISBN: 0-672-23281-2 $6.95

Do-it-yourselfer's step-by-step guide to interior remodeling with professional results: • general maintenance • wallboard installation and repair • wallboard taping • plaster repair • texture paints • wallpaper techniques • paneling • sound control • ceiling tile • bath tile • energy conservation.

Painting and Decorating
Rex Miller and Glenn E. Baker
5¹/₂ x 8¹/₄   Hardcover 464 pp.   325 illus.
ISBN: 0-672-23405-x $18.95

Practical guide for painters, decorators, and homeowners to the most up-to-date materials and techniques: • job planning • tools and equipment needed • finishing materials • surface preparation • applying paint and stains · decorating with coverings • repairs and maintenance • color and decorating principles.

VI

Tree Care ^{second edition}
John M. Haller
8½ x 11   Paperback   224 pp.   305 illus.
ISBN: 0-02-062870-6 $9.95

New edition of a standard in the field, for growers, nursery owners, foresters, landscapers, and homeowners: • planting • pruning • fertilizing • bracing and cabling • wound repair • grafting • spraying • disease and insect management • coping with environmental damage • removal • structure and physiology • recreational use.

Upholstering
updated
James E. Brumbaugh
5½ x 8¼   Hardcover   400 pp.   380 illus.
ISBN: 0-672-23372-x $12.95

Essentials of upholstering for professional, apprentice, and hobbyist: • furniture styles • tools and equipment • stripping • frame construction and repairs • finishing and refinishing wood surfaces • webbing • springs • burlap, stuffing, and muslin • pattern layout • cushions • foam padding • covers • channels and tufts • padded seats and slip seats • fabrics • plastics • furniture care.

Automotive and Engines

Diesel Engine Manual ^{fourth edition}
Perry O. Black; revised by William E. Scahill
5½ x 8¼   Hardcover   512 pp.   255 illus.
ISBN: 0-672-23371-1 $15.95

Detailed guide for mechanics, students, and others to all aspects of typical two- and four-cycle engines: • operating principles • fuel oil • diesel injection pumps • basic Mercedes diesels • diesel engine cylinders • lubrication • cooling systems • horsepower • engine-room procedures • diesel engine installation • automotive diesel engine • marine diesel engine • diesel electrical power plant • diesel engine service.

Gas Engine Manual ^{third edition}
Edwin P. Anderson; revised by Charles G. Facklam
5½ x 8¼   Hardcover   424 pp.   225 illus.
ISBN: 0-8161-1707-1 $12.95

Indispensable sourcebook for those who operate, maintain, and repair gas engines of all types and sizes: • fundamentals and classifications of engines · engine parts • pistons • crankshafts • valves • lubrication, cooling, fuel, ignition, emission

control and electrical systems • engine tune-up • servicing of pistons and piston rings, cylinder blocks, connecting rods and crankshafts, valves and valve gears, carburetors, and electrical systems.

Small Gasoline Engines
Rex Miller and Mark Richard Miller
5½ x 8¼   Hardcover   640 pp.   525 illus.
ISBN: 0-672-23414-9 $16.95

Practical information for those who repair, maintain, and overhaul two- and four-cycle engines – with emphasis on one-cylinder motors – including lawn mowers, edgers, grass sweepers, snowblowers, emergency electrical generators, outboard motors, and other equipment up to ten horsepower: • carburetors, emission controls, and ignition systems • starting systems • hand tools • safety • power generation • engine operations • lubrication systems • power drivers • preventive maintenance • step-by-step overhauling procedures • troubleshooting • testing and inspection • cylinder block servicing.

Truck Guide Library ^{3 vols}
James E. Brumbaugh
5½ x 8¼   Hardcover   2,144 pp.   1,715 illus.
ISBN: 0-672-23392-4 $45.95

Three-volume comprehensive and profusely illustrated reference on truck operation and maintenance.

Volume 1, Engines
5½ x 8¼   Hardcover   416 pp.   290 illus.
ISBN: 0-672-23356-8 $16.95

• Basic components · engine operating principles • troubleshooting • cylinder blocks • connecting rods, pistons, and rings • crankshafts, main bearings, and flywheels • camshafts and valve trains • engine valves.

Volume 2, Engine Auxiliary Systems
5½ x 8¼   Hardcover   704 pp.   520 illus.
ISBN: 0-672-23357-6 $16.95

• Battery and electrical systems • spark plugs • ignition systems, charging and starting systems • lubricating, cooling, and fuel systems • carburetors and governors • diesel systems • exhaust and emission-control systems.

Volume 3, Transmissions, Steering, and Brakes
5½ x 8¼   Hardcover   1,024 pp.   905 illus.
ISBN: 0-672-23406-8 $16.95

• Clutches • manual, auxiliary, and automatic transmissions • frame and suspension systems • differentials and axles, manual and power steering • front-end alignment • hydraulic, power, and air brakes • wheels and tires • trailers.

Drafting

Answers on Blueprint Reading
fourth edition
Roland E. Palmquist; revised by Thomas J. Morrisey
5½ x 8¼   Hardcover   320 pp.   275 illus.
ISBN: 0-8161-1704-7 $12.95

Complete question-and-answer instruction manual on blueprints of machines and tools, electrical systems, and architecture: • drafting scale • drafting instruments • conventional lines and representations • pictorial drawings • geometry of drafting • orthographic and working drawings • surfaces • detail drawing • sketching • map and topographical drawings • graphic symbols • architectural drawings • electrical blueprints • computer-aided design and drafting. Also included is an appendix of measurements • metric conversions • screw threads and tap drill sizes • number and letter sizes of drills with decimal equivalents • double depth of threads • tapers and angles.

Hobbies

Complete Course in Stained Glass
Pepe Mendez
8½ x 11   Paperback   80 pp.   50 illus.
ISBN: 0-672-23287-1 $8.95

Guide to the tools, materials, and techniques of the art of stained glass, with ten fully illustrated lessons: • how to cut glass • cartoon and pattern drawing • assembling and cementing • making lamps using various techniques • electrical components for completing lamps • sources of materials • glossary of terminology and techniques of stained glasswork.

Macmillan Practical Arts Library
Books for and by the Craftsman

World Woods in Color
W.A. Lincoln
7 × 10 Hardcover 300 pages
300 photos
ISBN: 0-02-572350-2 $39.95

Large full-color photographs show the natural grain and features of nearly 300 woods: • commercial and botanical names • physical characteristics, mechanical properties, seasoning, working properties, durability, and uses • the height, diameter, bark, and places of distribution of each tree • indexing of botanical, trade, commercial, local, and family names • a full bibliography of publications on timber study and identification.

The Woodturner's Art: Fundamentals and Projects
Ron Roszkiewicz
8 × 10 Hardcover 256 pages 300 illus.
ISBN: 0-02-605250-4 $24.95

A master woodturner shows how to design and create increasingly difficult projects step-by-step in this book suitable for the beginner and the more advanced student: • spindle and faceplate turning • tools • techniques • classic turnings from various historical periods • more than 30 types of projects including boxes, furniture, vases, and candlesticks • making duplicates • projects using combinations of techniques and more than one kind of wood. Author has also written *The Woodturner's Companion.*

The Woodworker's Bible
Alf Martensson
8 × 10 Paperback 288 pages 900 illus.
ISBN: 0-02-011940-2 $12.95

For the craftsperson familiar with basic carpentry skills, a guide to creating professional-quality furniture, cabinetry, and objects d'art in the home workshop: • techniques and expert advice on fine craftsmanship whether tooled by hand or machine • joint-making • assembling to ensure fit • finishes. Author, who lives in London and runs a workshop called Woodstock, has also written. *The Book of Furnituremaking.*

Cabinetmaking and Millwork
John L. Feirer
7⅛ × 9½ Hardcover 992 pages
2,350 illus. (32 pp. in color)
ISBN: 0-02-537350-1 $47.50

The classic on cabinetmaking that covers in detail all of the materials, tools, machines, and processes used in building cabinets and interiors, the production of furniture, and other work of the finish carpenter and millwright: • fixed installations such as paneling, built-ins, and cabinets • movable wood products such as furniture and fixtures • which woods to use, and why and how to use them in the interiors of homes and commercial buildings • metrics and plastics in furniture construction.

Cabinetmaking: The Professional Approach
Alan Peters
8½ × 11 Hardcover 208 pages 175 illus. (8 pp. color)
ISBN: 0-02-596200-0 $29.95

A unique guide to all aspects of professional furniture making, from an English master craftsman: • the Cotswold School and the birth of the furniture movement • setting up a professional shop • equipment • finance and business efficiency • furniture design • working to commission • batch production, training, and techniques • plans for nine projects.

Carpentry and Building Construction
John L. Feirer and Gilbert R. Hutchings
7½ × 9½ hardcover 1,120 pages
2,000 photos (8 pp. in color)
ISBN: 0-02-537360-9 $50.00

A classic by Feirer on each detail of modern construction: • the various machines, tools, and equipment from which the builder can choose • laying of a foundation • building frames for each part of a building • details of interior and exterior work • painting and finishing • reading plans • chimneys and fireplaces • ventilation • assembling prefabricated houses.